SELF IMAGE

Raaj Sinha

BlueRose ONE.com
Stories Matter
NewDelhi • London

BLUEROSE PUBLISHERS
India | U.K.

BlueRose ONE.com
Stories Matter
NewDelhi • London

For permissions requests or inquiries regarding this publication, please contact:

BLUEROSE PUBLISHERS
www.BlueRoseONE.com
info@bluerosepublishers.com
+91 8882 898 898
+4407342408967

ISBN: 978-93-7542-888-6

Cover design: Aman
Typesetting: Tanya Raj Upadhyay

First Edition: January 2025

A Way to a Dream Life

Acknowledgements

I would like to express my heartfelt gratitude to the Almighty for blessing me with wonderful parents whose unwavering support has shaped me into the person I am today.

A special thank you to my spiritual Guru, Sri Sri Ravi Shankar, whose teachings have ignited a profound quest for knowledge within me, guiding my thoughts and actions.

To my loving wife, Bandita, your support during all circumstances has been my anchor and source of strength. My daughter, Siyona, you are not just my child but a true teacher, illuminating my life with joy and wisdom each day.

I sincerely appreciate my colleagues in the corporate world who have fostered a positive and progressive environment, especially during challenging projects. Your encouragement and support have been invaluable.

I am also thankful to all my friends, family, and acquaintances who have believed in me. Your faith has motivated me to persevere.

To everyone with whom I have interacted throughout my journey, thank you for the insights and life lessons you have shared — they have enriched my understanding and perspective immensely.

Finally, my deepest thanks go to the new community of readers and all those who believed in my work and chose to purchase this book. Your support means the world to me, and I hope this book resonates with you as much as your belief has inspired me.

I offer my sincere gratitude to all the co-creators of life's force on this planet who have guided humanity toward a better life.

Thank you all!

Preface

In our daily lives, it is common to get wrapped up in our routines and lose sight of our real targets. Often, we may not realise until much later whether we are truly headed in the right direction. Even when making bigger decisions about our careers, our children's education, or personal goals, we often rely on cues from our surroundings and the subconscious mind prompts to determine our path forward. While we tend to focus our efforts on external influences, we often overlook the inner prompt that guides us. It may be worth considering how we can harness this internal guidance to make more justified and informed decisions about our future.

Our inner voice plays a critical role in our decision-making process throughout our lives. It functions as a judge, offering guidance on whether to pursue a goal or not. This guidance is essential in shaping our actions and determining the outcome of our endeavours.

Our ability to achieve our daily targets is often influenced by various factors that affect our thought processes and the inner prompt. Two significant factors affecting this inner prompt are our environment and our self-image. Self-image is the source that provides the internal prompts—most of the time, subconsciously. While our surroundings determine the areas in which we set our goals, our self-image determines the level of our goals and our ability to achieve them.

It is common for us to adopt the thought process of our surroundings, which can limit us in ways we may not even realise. Despite this limitation, we often feel safe following the majority and leading a relatively secure life, or so to say. However, when we encounter life lessons from enlightened sources such as scriptures, knowledge books, and motivational speeches, we may find it difficult to apply them in our daily lives. It can be challenging to break free from our established ways of thinking and working, causing us to revert to our old habits ultimately.

In today's world, people prioritise quick results over everything else, especially the younger generation. We rush to achieve our targets, and in the process, we tend to ignore the fundamental attitudes and behaviours that we were taught during our early years in school and consider them as obstacles to our growth. We follow the crowd and later realise that our pursuit of targets kept us so busy that we couldn't live the happy life we had once envisioned. Thus, our dreams remain unfulfilled.

Pursuing success without finding oneself and without developing fundamental attributes can negatively affect one's mental well-being. Bringing these two into one's life can provide a sense of direction and help establish a strong personal identity. Learning how to live a fulfilling life can promote positivity and prevent feelings of unhappiness. One may note that material success alone may not bring meaning to one's life if these fundamental attributes are absent.

This book attempts to approach this challenge in a different but refreshing way. Unveiling a new side of you, that was invisible to you until now—the original 'you' when you came to this planet. This is presented in a framework that makes the unveiling process easy to adopt and practice. This helps to cut through the confusion and face life head-on to achieve ultimate success and happiness.

The ideas presented in this book are based on various challenging experiences encountered throughout life. These experiences often involve complex interactions and navigating difficult situations with others. The pursuit of effective solutions for life and career challenges has led to the exploration of multiple resources, including books on psychology, philosophy, history, science and self-help. It is evident that there is a huge amount of knowledge available for personal development, yet misconceptions and erroneous beliefs persist.

The process of self-development itself is considered a painful process, and many who want to tread this path drop midway through the journey because their mind is unable to accept new changes.

Through this book, I have attempted to make the concepts clear, interesting, and result-oriented at each step. The attempt is also made to give the process a visual effect inside your mind, making the concept easy to comprehend.

Short stories have been used to fortify concepts and clarify them wherever necessary. Questions/Exercises have been presented at the end of the chapter to make it more interactive and participative.

I hope this book will ignite the spark you have been waiting for in your life.

Table of Contents

Chapter 1
Introduction

Why do we work tirelessly day in and day out but still fall short of our dreams? Why does it feel like inner peace is a thing of the past? We all want to achieve success and lasting happiness, but how do we make it happen? How can we become individuals who add real value to society? Why is it that we go through inspiring stories and listen to lectures but still fail to measure up when it comes to achieving success and happiness? The answers to these questions are out there, spread in several pieces. Therefore, the challenge lies in putting the pieces in the correct sequence.

My new journey began with the quest to understand why I hadn't achieved something more impactful or substantial in my life while working for so many years. Why did I fear stepping into the unknown and, therefore, keep making compromises with my dreams? How can somebody become truly successful at a relatively younger age while the majority struggle to make ends meet? These questions led to various answers that never convinced me, like: work hard, stay focused, be truthful, plan your life and each day, believe in God, be courageous, be fearless, be resilient, be disciplined and much more.

Logically, I have seen several people who work hard, are efficient in their skills, are resilient, disciplined or have several good attributes, and still lead an average, painful life. Therefore, something else must be there that I am missing.

For a significant part of my life, I thought success required a sharp mind —a God's gift that propels some on a different trajectory of success while others struggle. But many sharp minds lead average lives, while average individuals achieve tremendous success. How is it so?

Many of us are constantly searching for the key to happiness and success. We often try different things and products that promise to make us happy. However, it's like solving a jigsaw puzzle without the right pieces. Without correct knowledge, we chase success for happiness and end up with almost nothing in return. We ultimately have to lower our goals and targets, settling for a compromised life.

The reason for a compromised life is in the thinking process. The frame or ambit of our thinking limits our potential. Unless we change our thinking process, our mind cannot step out to think differently than it has been doing to date.

Changing the frame of our thinking mind is a different journey altogether. Building a new structure on an existing frame already limited by design is not the right approach. Instead, we should dismantle the old frame and build a new one.

This book is about building a new frame of mind through a step-by-step process. It first explains how we subconsciously build our present mental frame and why it limits us from achieving the things we desire. Then, it gives you the step-by-step process of building a new frame to think, plan, and execute suitable and more significant goals in life with ease, peace, and happiness.

Also, we realize that success is not a one-time occurrence but a culture we bring into our lives. The image that we build for ourselves brings happiness and success with ease. The steps for transformation in this book do not require a high level of education, talent, or good fortune. This book is for anyone wanting to transform their lives and achieve their dreams.

I do not have a suave writing style or knowledge of English to impress you. Therefore, the book is written in simple language— the way we talk— except where I have attempted to use some classy stuff that fascinates me when I hear them.

If you follow the sequence narrated in the book and have unflinching faith in the process, you will transform into a role model for others to follow. Eventually, leading your life to the fullest, making the best use of your inner resources and attaining a sense of purpose, harmony and fulfilment.

For students: The book will enlighten you on balancing your energy between academic requirements and developing your self-image, setting you on the path to acquiring crucial practical life skills.

For parents: Read the book with equal fervour, become a pillar of great support in your child's journey of success, and possibly begin your own.

For professionals: Apply the steps to achieve maximum success in your business or job.

It's simple. It's the law. You cannot circumvent it if you want to achieve success and happiness.

After understanding the guiding principles, you will set the blueprint for your success. The framework for leading your dream life.

"There is nothing better than having a feeling of a life well lived."

Raaj Sinha

You have taken the most significant step of your life by laying your hands on this book. Now, read it with deep faith. Pledge to finish it within a week. Complete all the exercises and note significant learnings.

I suggest reading this book several times to engrain the principles and concepts discussed here deeply. They should become a part of your everyday life.

A word of Caution:

You will be on a new journey in your life. You may be required to let go:

1. Your old, non-progressive friends and acquaintances.
2. Habits of wasting time.
3. Your current self-image will be replaced by the one that leads you to acquire the character and skills of an achiever. You will be making new friends and acquaintances that align with your goals.

Chapter 2
My Realization

From an early age, I've felt a strong inner desire to engage more deeply with society and its most pressing needs. The relentless pursuit of a better existence has always fascinated me, particularly matters of the human psyche. Delving into the human psyche, my mind could travel to different spaces and times and see people living blissfully in those realms.

Despite this enduring desire, I was yet to take meaningful steps in that direction, leaving me with constant unease and dissatisfaction.

However, despite the thoughts surrounding me, an unsettling whisper lingered in my mind, reminding me that what I envisioned was perhaps nothing more than a figment of my imagination. I realized it was pointless to dwell on these unrealistic dreams; after all, the society that shaped my upbringing valued practicality above all else, emphasizing the relentless struggle to earn a living over pursuing artistic passions.

For most of my life, I lived according to what I believed society expected of me. I was constantly striving for an identity that society seemed to reward, all the while not being certain of who I truly was or what I wanted out of life. Looking back on it now, it's strange to think I was pursuing what others considered important.

I often felt a lack of ease in my everyday life. I felt like I was always searching for something I couldn't quite identify, racing against time to find it. However, this approach wasn't working and only contributed to my irritability and stubbornness.

During the COVID-19 lockdown, we were confined to our homes for the first time. However, our offices needed to continue operating as usual. Our organization was new, and we had to establish systems and processes with a fresh team. This led to working late into the evening and having little time to spend with my family.

Two incidents happened that changed the course of my life:

One day during an afternoon break, exhausted, I stepped towards my washroom door. However, my mind suddenly went blank, and an inexplicable shift occurred. I felt I was bridging two realms—the moment transitioning from the mundane reality I knew to a breathtaking world that unfolded before me.

In this stunning alternate reality, vibrant hues danced in the air, enveloped by a symphony of captivating melodies. The landscape was a feast for the senses, filled with intricate artworks that seemed to pulse with life. It was a realm that mirrored the wild imaginings I had cradled in my heart yet never witnessed in the confines of my daily existence. My conscience told me, "See, all that you imagined is actually a reality. You were not wrong in your imagination."

Time slipped away in that mesmerizing space, and after what felt like a blissful eternity—ten minutes, to be precise—I was abruptly pulled back to the stark reality that awaited me. When I opened my eyes, I found myself lying on the bed in my familiar surroundings, where my family stood around me, their faces etched with panic and despair. Tears streamed down their cheeks as they helplessly called out to me, a stark contrast to the vibrant world I had just left behind. For them, I was senseless.

That day, I couldn't sleep at night. A realization dawned upon me. I felt I needed to do more meaningful things in life and pursue my dreams.

During the same period, another incident occurred; I observed that my daughter had developed some habits that may not help her later in life, such as mindlessly watching TV or long chats with friends. Whenever I noticed these things or saw her doing them, I expressed annoyance and told her these may not help her later in life.

One day, while conversing with my wife about our daughter's habits, my daughter unexpectedly joined the discussion. She looked at me and compassionately expressed, "Papa, I understand the need to put in more effort and improve. I promise to work on it gradually. However, your constant pressure and nagging aren't helping. It's beginning to feel a bit suffocating. Please try not to worry too much."

Her words struck a chord in me. I realized that I had become a grouch. All these years, I took pride in my critical intelligence. I attributed my success—whatever I had—to my ability to find gaps and say no. I realised for the first time that looking at the positive aspects, encouraging them, and developing them is better than just looking on the wrong side.

These revelations caused me to reflect on my life's direction. I asked myself important questions: where was my life headed? Am I leading a happy and peaceful life? What value am I creating for the society? Have I lived my life to my fullest potential? How much money have I saved for myself and my family? It became clear that I had missed out on several things

I had planned for my life when I was young. I realised that my involvement with my job had distanced me from my true objective of serving society. I had lost sight of my original goals while trying to prove my worth to society.

I realized I had never thought about where my life was heading. Was I leading a purposeful life? I sensed that I was running to achieve a goal that would not give me ultimate peace and satisfaction. It became evident that all my hard work was not in the right direction. I chose a path in the beginning that would not give me real pleasure. I hadn't planned my journey from beginning to end, leaving me stuck in the mindless chase.

Recalling the lines from A.E Houseman's poetry: 'Yonder see the morning blink'

> The sun is up, and up must I,
>
> To wash and dress and eat and drink
>
> And look at things and talk and think
>
> And work, and God knows why.
>
> Oh often have I washed and dressed
>
> And what's to show for all my pain?
>
> Let me lie abed and rest:
>
> Ten thousand times I've done my best
>
> And all's to do again.

The poem likely conveys the importance of having a goal in life. Without a goal, every day may feel like a meaningless chore, and even if you work hard, you won't feel the true joy of life.

I, too, realized that if I do not lead my life as I had dreamed, I may end up being selfish and unfulfilled.

I realized I needed to take certain actions quickly to put myself on the right path. I read many books and articles, searched my soul, and attended lectures by prominent people from both the spiritual and material world. I devised a way to live a life of success, peace, and happiness. From those learnings, I devised some of the principles for transforming life, began writing and started living by them. These principles guide me to live the rest of my life with greater fulfilment. When I started practising these principles, I found the joy I had been yearning for all these years.

I often encounter people who question why I want to pursue my goals at this stage of my life, saying, "You're already doing well. Why do you seem dissatisfied?" While my financial goals were okay, though not terrific, my happiness was suffering. My relationship quotient was not great; my mental and physical well-being was not in good shape. Also, my inner desire to be of direct use to society was not being achieved. I needed to align myself with the desired outputs. My discontent with my current situation did not indicate something was wrong with me but rather a sign that I needed to become the person I constantly desired.

It's never too late to be who you might have been

George Elliot

"I am going to lead my life in my way. It will make me happy to know I have done the work I was sent to do."

Raaj Sinha

I realized that it's not prudent to be knowledgeable about several things in life.

You will do enough good for yourself and society if you focus on one thing, live with it in your breath day and night, and 'let go' of the rest of the things happening around you.

Also important is to expand your context. It will allow you to see new horizons

- You grow only when you serve.
- You succeed only when you help others succeed.
- The bigger the community you serve, the bigger purpose you serve.
- Not taking risks will leave us being average, and the average is a failing formula in life.

I wish I had this book in my teens; I would have avoided a lot of stress, misery and dullness in my life. I would have been more focused on my journey. It would have been useful when I graduated from college or even in my mid-20s. This is the book I need now, as life's principles for attaining success don't change.

My goal is to tell people the key to true success in life, which academia often fails to do: how to lead a happy life. I missed this during my early and mid-prime and want to ensure that others don't make the same mistake.

Chapter 3
Youth's Dilemma

Many young individuals are uncertain about their career paths even after completing a college degree. This uncertainty is often compounded by a negative self-image that develops over time, influenced by discouraging feedback from authority figures and peers. As a result, these young adults may experience limitations in their critical thinking and decision-making abilities, making it challenging for them to envision and pursue fulfilling careers.

These minds are already in survival mode, searching for an opportunity to get to a rescue platform in their lives. Anything that promises them a rescue path brings hope to these youths. Unable to think about what suits them, they look around, see what others are doing, and follow that. Even though their subconscious mind expresses reservations about pursuing the path, it gets suppressed by the looming fear of an uncertain future. Therefore, they take the most known route, though they may feel uncomfortable inside. The pressure of securing the future by parents and society is so great that they just follow other's suggestions. They somehow scramble to get a job, only to find out later that securing the future is an illusion. Later, they find themselves stuck in their daily routines, making it difficult to escape the grind.

The fact is that the track of hopelessness and despair is sown in school. Whether you like it or not, you must prove your understanding of the knowledge gained at school by appearing for exams. After secondary schooling, students who see limited options opt for a professional degree. No matter your interests, you first need to become a doctor, engineer or an MBA, and then later, if you have the flair and courage, you can step into some other profession or start a business.

Parents invest several billion dollars (thousands of crores in Indian rupees) in coaching institutes to prepare their children for the entrance exams. Most students' eventual fate is a disappointment. They are trying for something they haven't developed a liking for, but parents and societal pressure force them into this uncanny situation.

PS: *Many successful students do not pursue something they are passionate about but get into professional courses to secure their future and earn a better living. They devote their lives to doing the job without being passionate about it, just for their livelihood or the extra money they get.*

When these students enter adulthood, their self-image becomes a bit complex. They acquire the mental frame that thinks: 1. Get a degree to find a better job. 2. Doing a job and enjoying life are two different things poles apart. Therefore, three weeks of holidaying are for enjoyment, and the remaining days of the year chew the bitter pill every day of being stuck in an uncomfortable job situation to serve the family.

They also realize that only a small portion of what they studied during college is being applied in their present job roles. This has led to the mindset that knowledge is hardly useful; getting good grades is all that is important for securing a better future.

The crisis starts midway into their careers when they struggle to progress further. They realize they need different skills, often referred to as soft skills, behavioural skills, and leadership skills, which we will call 'practical life skills', which become vital for further progress. They also need to be creative to take their company to new heights. But by this time, they would have lost the battle internally for learning something new to improve their position. Their self-image would not allow them to inherit these traits and increase their goal targets.

The fundamental ways of living a happy, responsible and successful life never change. However, our minds change based on what we observe and experience. The mindset we acquire from our limited ecosystem complicates our lives.

It is necessary to change our mindset to acquire a high self-image. A high self-image also reflects a strong character. It enables the person to discover oneself and find a suitable career without spending a lot of time and effort in the wrong direction.

These individuals will become responsible members of society and the nation and contribute significantly to shaping a better culture. They will have great energy and influence and be acknowledged in their fields.

Empty yourself

Keeping an open mind when learning to build new concepts and knowledge is essential. If you go in with preconceived notions and judge things based on what you already know, you may miss out on valuable information. The flow of knowledge cannot get into a cup that is already full or inverted.

Therefore, **empty yourself.**

I know this isn't easy, but remember, the best learner is one who dedicates himself to the task in front, with all sincerity, without procrastinating.

A small story…

Blank paper

A priest came to a guru, a spiritual master. The priest was very popular, even more famous than the guru, and had great knowledge of the scriptures. Despite knowing the scriptures by heart, he felt incomplete. He could recall words but could not find the door to reach the wordless silence.

So, he looked for a guru in the decisive moments of life. He did find one. The guru looked at the priest and said, "So, I see a lot of obstacles within you! Your knowledge is overwhelming. Write down all you know and bring it to me. Why talk about whatever you already know? We will leave all that aside. I will then tell you what you don't know."

The disciple left and returned after a year with a thousand-page book. The guru said, "You've come back! I wasn't sure if you could come back because so much information was in your head. I didn't know how long it would take."

Seeing the thousand-page book, the master said, "This is too much. I am old now; my death is near. I cannot read so much. Write it all down in brief. Just bring me the gist of it."

After three months, the priest returned with 100 pages. The master said, "This, too, is a lot. My days are numbered; bring it down even more."

The disciple then summarised everything on a single page and returned. The guru was nearing death. He said, "Brother, this is too much. Make it even more concise. Go to the next room and quickly summarize it." The disciple wrote the whole essence in a single sentence, a hymn.

The guru was holding his last breath and said, "I'm holding on for you. When will you understand? Make it even shorter. Why are you being a miser with making it brief?" Then, the disciple came to his senses. He ran to the other room and brought back a blank paper to the guru.

The master said, "You have become a disciple! Although I am leaving, your relationship with me will continue. When I was alive, we had no connection, as knowledge stood in between us. But now you have emptied yourself. Now, you have become a blank paper. Don't worry; our relationship is established, and death will not be able to break it. Life could not have connected us in the same way as this."

In that moment of emptiness, the disciple attained divinity.

What happened when he brought the blank paper?

Bringing the blank paper meant being empty from within!

This is the first thing we must do before preparing to gain knowledge and become truly successful and happy. Free yourself from your past knowledge, experience and bindings. Believe that you are going to experience something new.

Teenagers and young adults bubble with energy and enthusiasm, but it is primarily untamed. They do not relate to people who do not exhibit a similar kind of energy. Moreover, they are experiencing new things in life, making them excited to follow or explore. They are on FastTrack mode to do what they have heard or seen. Sometimes, it becomes difficult for them to adopt new things that were not on their agenda initially. But gradually, they accept new learning. Therefore, I want to emphasize them for being empty, as well.

Here's one more citing of being empty from within.

The following story is derived from the Bhagavata Purana. According to the tale, Radha, Lord Krishna's beloved, became incredibly envious of his constant companionship with his flute. Once, she asked Krishna, "Why do you always keep this flute on your lips? You don't even spend as much time with me as you do with this flute. What is the reason behind this?" However, Krishna would smile in response.

One day, Radha became so jealous of the flute that she broke it open to see what was inside. To her surprise, she found that the flute was empty. Similarly, to experience divinity, we must remove everything undesirable and develop absolute emptiness. If God has to play that divine music like the flute through our hearts, then we must clear our hearts of unwanted desires, thoughts, impurities and complexities. Just like a flute needs to be empty to produce melodious music, we must empty ourselves to receive proper knowledge and happiness.

Chapter 4
What is Success

Until now, we have discussed the present education system's inability to provide the life we want, probably because the foundation it builds inside us is not based on basic life fundamentals. We learn to desperately chase someone else's copied or borrowed goals without understanding our lives and the true meaning of happiness or success. Since the book's theme is about leading one's dream life, let's first define success before we move forward.

One can define success as achieving the desired outcome.

Your idea of success may vary depending on your current situation, surroundings and experiences. For most middle-class individuals, success usually means having a stable job, owning a home or car, financial stability, and providing their children with a good education. However, have you ever considered the cost of achieving these things? Your family spends all their energy to earn enough money to satisfy these desires. Your children are in daycare while you are busy working. You may not have enough time to spend with your loved ones or pursue hobbies. You may have to save up for an entire year for a two-week vacation. All of these factors lead to decreased engagement and satisfaction in life. You must pause and reflect on your situation. You did not come into this world solely to work and earn money to meet your ends.

Besides just earning, there are other objectives in life that should be fulfilled to attain true happiness. Therefore, to achieve true happiness through success, you must do so in a holistic manner. Success can be achieved in many realms: wealth, career, family, spirituality, health, knowledge, and contribution to the community or a combination of these. But a feeling of completeness comes when our deep-down desires are satiated. Nowadays, we are just working on the surface to earn more money to meet our ends, and, therefore, we cannot get the desired results even after working so hard. Let's pause and think about it.

Most of us need help understanding the whole process of success, and we only keep citing successful people's biographies as motivational stories to our children and to our community. We read the biographies of successful people, and they hardly impact our lives. They just remain in our memory as stories.

Some people are inspired by them, enrol in a self-development program, and start a new habit. But sooner or later, they give up midway and return to where they started, with a negative feeling towards themselves or the program.

We fail to understand why it didn't work for us. How does it work for those who are successful?

Success needs to be a regular phenomenon. It cannot happen once or twice in a lifetime. To reach the next level, we must outgrow ourselves every time we achieve the set target. We need to keep growing; that is life.

If you want a perfectly healthy body, can you achieve it once in a lifetime? You may get out of shape or become unfit in a few months. The same is valid with success. Maintaining and growing further will take the same kind of consistent effort. Therefore, success is a culture that gets into our habits.

The biggest motivator for achieving success is that you will be able to spend more quality time with yourself and your loved ones. You will feel good most of the time, be physically and mentally fit, and be positive and high on energy. You will be able to contribute to society's well-being, and society will value you. True success comes to those whose fundamental attributes are strong, as they keep them grounded.

A Kite Story:

Once, a six-year-old child asked his father, "Dad... what is a successful life?"

The father smiled at his son and replied, "Why do you like flying kites?" The child replied excitedly, "I love seeing kites flying high in the sky."

The father said, "Let us go and fly kites." They both went to the roof of their house to fly kites. Both father and son got engrossed in kites and enjoyed a lot.

After a while, the son said to his father, "Dad... the kite is not able to go higher because of the string, shall we break it? The kite will go even higher."

At the child's behest, the father broke the string...the kite went a little higher... and after that, it came down, waving, and fell to a distant location.

The son got upset and asked his father, "Why did the kite fall?"

Father smiled and taught his son a valuable life lesson. He compared the kite's flight to our own aspirations and desires. “The string that holds the kite doesn't hinder its ascent; it actually provides support, just like our own attachments keep us grounded and help us maintain our position. Instead of severing ties with these threads, we should nurture them with love and care. Balancing our attachments, like a kite and its string, is what constitutes a truly successful life."

A life well lived

As children, we all dream big, but as we grow into adults, we often refine our targets and lead compromised lives. Our parents, who initially supported our dreams, changed their stance, and all their efforts are directed at making our lives secure. Once we start moving towards securing our lives, we never realise that our whole life slips under us, and we hardly know a way to get out of it or change our paths. The entire concept of securing ourselves is an illusion that we never realise. Most of us do not become happy by truly securing ourselves. Still, we lower our targets to achieve them with comfort and gain a sense of happiness, albeit for a short duration. Some realize this in old age, while others may leave this world without realizing it. The feeling of "Probably, I have not lived my life to the fullest or the way I would have wanted" makes you uncomfortable or sad. You might hear from your parents or elders close to you saying, "Had I done this, I would have become this or would have achieved that", and so on.

But somehow, we get caught up in a never-ending cycle of work, spend, and work some more. We experience short-lived moments of joy and an overwhelming long period of boredom and sadness.

We never realise that we are born not to chase money but to live life to our fullest capacity. We learn from our surroundings that leading a happy life is by earning a lot of money. Therefore, in the quest for money, we may find that either we do not get it, or if we do, it robs us of true happiness. Also, in this pursuit, much time slips away from our precious life.

Why live with that pang of regret later in life?

Live your life to the fullest now, with no pain or no regrets later.

So, what would be a fulfilling life?

A fulfilling life comprises:

1. Knowing your life's purpose: Align your dreams to add value to yourself and others.
2. Living your passion: Break out of your comfort zone and find pursuits you love from your heart and positively impact the world around you.
3. Lead by example: Show consistency in your actions and behaviour at home or work. Develop a character that is consistently reliable and helpful to others.
4. Give back: Take whatever you can from life, but always give back. One of the most fulfilling feelings you get in life is serving others. Throughout our lives, we have to rely on society for every accomplishment we achieve. Whether it's the education, the job we do, or the services we use, society plays a crucial role in our lives. Therefore, our moral obligation is to give back to society and contribute to its well-being.
5. Nurture relationships: Possessions are not a source of lasting happiness. Your legacy will be the relationships you build and the lives you impact.
6. Keep improving: Strive to improve every day than you were yesterday.
7. Stay Healthy; uplift your mind, body and soul.
8. Spend quality time with your loved ones

Exercise:

1. What does a successful life comprise?

___

___

___

2. Where are you compromising in your life? List it out. Find out the reasons.

___

___

___

3. Nurture your attachments with love and care. Express your thoughts on how you would do that.

___

___

___

Chapter 5
A Painful Fallacy

When we ask our children to be disciplined, our parents often tell us not to push them, to let them be on their own and enjoy life. They ask, "How disciplined were you at this age?"

However, after a certain age, children must be disciplined to lead a better life. Discipline is a way of life, so why not become disciplined early?

It is essential to discipline children at an early age. It is like a tree that needs guides on its sides to grow straight and tall. Providing the right environment and early support helps the tree grow strong. If not, the tree may not grow big and straight. You may have to redo the process correctly. This metaphor implies that if children are not disciplined from a young age, they may not develop good character traits and values, which could affect their future. It is crucial to guide and support children in their early years to help them grow into responsible and successful adults.

The other half of Academics

The middle-class society in India often lives in dreams, many of which remain unfulfilled. Therefore, they put their maximum effort into educating their children, hoping that their children will one day achieve what they couldn't. They sincerely put in consistent effort to help with the child's homework, pay high school fees, relocate to ensure better education opportunities, attend parent-teacher meetings, observe the child's academic progress, etc. Almost their entire life revolves around their children's academics.

Apart from regular classes, parents enrol their children in extra tuition classes so that children improve their knowledge in particular subjects and ultimately fare well in exams.

Additionally, many parents enrol their children in extracurricular activities such as sports, dance, singing, drama, and games. Some parents believe these activities will improve their child's physical and mental health and overall outlook. However, most parents enrol their children in these activities out of fear of falling behind others, without focusing on the overall outcome. As a result, they remain merely engaged.

Schools also encourage and emphasise children's participation in such activities. However, they do not link them to student performance, as the education system is tuned to see only academic excellence.

So much involvement without a focused approach does not yield the required result because they don't know exactly where to focus and how much impetus to give it.

Parents' effort and dedication continue until their child gets a job. For a parent, their children getting a job is like the culmination of the effort they have put in for years.

Voila! Can you believe this? Sixteen years of a parent's life is focused on a child's academics, and hardly anything matches this priority. But did you know that your approach towards your child's future is already in survival mode? Therefore, it is highly likely that they would attain a living for survival. You may ask, "Then what have we missed?" The answer is simple: You have focussed only on one half of making your child successful and ignored the other half!

Two halves make your education complete. The academic curriculum taught in school is only one part. The other is about applying practical skills. Parents are often unaware that their focus on seeing their child excel in their career is missing the planning and preparation for the second half of education and how it will affect their child's outcome. With the lack of education in the second part, many students feel stressed out when their growth path is restricted at some point in their career (for the majority at the initial phase), and their original dreams remain unfulfilled.

We never realized that the one-end merited education system, which consumes the best sixteen years of our lives, doesn't make us successful. They may, at best, help land a good job. Initially, getting hooked up by a company after completing a degree might make us feel elated then, but what happens as an outcome after you settle down in your life, say after ten or fifteen years? Life becomes stressful. You are unable to meet your desires. In office, you see your progress rate slowed down as you grow up the ladder and opportunities taper down. Subconsciously, you compromise your dreams and decide to remain mediocre. Your targets and desires become smaller.

Sadly, after so much effort to help children excel in exams, parents and children make a heavy compromise. This compromise is gradual and happens subconsciously. Therefore, the pain isn't immediate. Children tread the same line as parents did, leading to similar outcomes. It is no surprise that they end up being average. Parents may feel good about providing better amenities than they had. But this is true for everyone. The next generation always leads a better life (amenities-wise). Whatever amenities your child gets are attainable by a significant population nowadays. The previous generation struggled to buy a house or car of their own. Now, almost everybody has it. This is a generation shift or generation norm. We are living in the best of times in human civilization, amenity-wise.

But we are also a lot more stressed. Anne Halen Petersen noted in the book 'Can't Even' how the new generation has become stressed due to the present culture of striving. Are these conditions making them successful and happy? Is work with severe stress becoming a part of the new culture?

Some of you may argue that I am casting an opposing view. However, I am not trying to be negative. Instead, I intend to help you realize the effort you put in and its actual outcome. Let's look at the complete perspective of the outcome. Did your parents put in the same kind of effort? Even if they did, the opportunities available to them were limited at that time. In the past, most people who earned a degree could find a job with job security and a handsome pension after retirement. Children's education was less expensive, and expenditures on healthcare were minimal. There were neither many avenues to spend money nor as many desires to fulfil. People could easily afford to bring up three to four kids. However, now things are different. Bringing up one or two children is stressful as desires far exceed our earnings. Jobs are no longer guaranteed for life, as most are privately owned. Any changes in the company's performance or a downturn in the sector in which your company works can affect your position or job. Life has become more stressful and manipulative.

Education and healthcare have become very expensive. Moreover, the middle class is stretching itself to lead a better lifestyle. Owning a house, car, costly gadgets at home, exotic vacations, expenditures on maintaining health, and dining out have increased manyfold.

With this kind of inflation and lifestyle changes, predicting the cost of a good lifestyle in the coming fifteen years can be more challenging.

Things are rapidly changing around us. Now, we are in 'The information age'. All knowledge is at our fingertips. Our educational degrees won't matter much here, but skills and efficiency are crucial. You will be left far behind without knowing what to pick up for your success because others may be tapping at the right point in this vast information pipeline and bringing knowledge into action. Those will be the successful lot.

Parents guide their children to the best of their understanding. A common understanding is that if your kids do well in exams, then they will be successful in their lives. But this is ignorance. Mere success in exams doesn't make their life successful. Will getting a job give them a dream life? It is only the beginning. So, how can our kids have a life that is on a different trajectory from their parents? This is something unknown to you; therefore, you are oblivious.

This is because our ecosystem (the society we live in and interact with people) may not provide the perspective required to understand this.

Let me ask a few questions: Task no.1: How many successful people have you met? How many of these personalities have you studied in detail, especially about how they achieved their success?

Again, our education system does not teach you all that. It only talks a bit about the journey and achievements of these great or successful people. We are taught about these personalities and their hardships, but we do not emphasise adopting them in our lives. Still, without emulating all those traits, you can be adjudged the best student in your class. And we are unable to look beyond that.

Since we were superficially taught about the traits and character of these great personalities, it never impacted us beyond the surface of our conscience.

Now, Task no.2: Find out who stood first in your class in the 10th or 12th exam. And what have they achieved in their lives? You may do this at the end of this chapter.

Task no. 3: Find three 'great achievers', go through their life journey, and understand what has helped them achieve great success.

I've observed the career journeys of many exceptional students, including my wife, the top-performing student in her school. However, when these students enter the practical world, they often encounter various challenges. Their success in navigating these challenges depends on their abilities and the support they receive from their environment. These students must understand and prepare for the skills necessary to excel in their practical journey.

Unfortunately, these 'practical life skills' require good observation and equal or more dedication. However, most grade-A students find it challenging to learn these skills due to their past acknowledgements, giving them a false sense of being ahead of the race. But later, they realize they are missing something that doesn't allow them to ride on that high-speed corridor of success with true happiness. But by the time they realise this, the feeling of helplessness sets in them. They would need the right mindset to find that piece of the jigsaw puzzle they did not possess until now.

This concerns a section of those who excel academically but struggle to adapt to new requirements. However, what about those students who, for some reason, could not achieve good grades in their exams? Society tends to view them as second or even third-class citizens, affecting their self-esteem and, ultimately, their career prospects. Despite this, many continue to strive to achieve better grades to secure a better future for themselves but often end up living a compromised life.

A student's life in India can be imagined as participating in a swimming competition in an open river without knowing if they love swimming. You think there is hardly any sport other than swimming, so you must learn. You learn a bit about swimming in a controlled environment and are made to appear in the competition. You begin swimming in the river without knowing the challenges you face ahead. After swaying some distance, you realize that challenges are coming in several ways. The water current is strong and has become murkier, making swimming difficult. You pray to God to give you enough strength to reach the shore safely. Some even drown in the river and end their life. Others somehow gather the courage to reach the shore, exhausted and battered. You realize the competition results don't matter as much as surviving the ordeal. Every year, tens of thousands of students suffer from this fear of taking the plunge by compulsion. All this works negatively for the self-image of a large number of individuals.

Working with large conglomerates, I had the opportunity to observe and interact with both high academic achievers and the lesser-considered lot. Generally, high academic achievers start with high self-confidence as they gain a better position initially. But in the long run, success includes people from both circles.

You will notice that some of them, who were not so good at academics, have done well in business or jobs due to their 'practical life skills', which stemmed from a high self-image. They were the real dark horses.

Here, I should clarify that I don't mean to say that people with excellent academic records do not have practical life skills. Rather, they are more likely to succeed because of their discipline, grit, and sense of past accomplishments. Therefore, those who are prepared for new challenges and adapt quickly become super achievers in their field.

Obtaining good grades in exams helps start a career positively. However, practical skills are crucial for long-term success. Unfortunately, many people struggle to develop these skills due to the negative self-image they have built for such attributes within themselves. They often think, "It's not meant for me", and then subconsciously reject it.

The key to acquiring practical life skills is to start with a solid foundation of life's fundamental skills. Without these fundamentals, it would be challenging to perform well under pressure. Therefore, it's essential to focus on acquiring them first. Once you develop these fundamental skills, you'll gain more confidence in yourself and your abilities, boosting your self-esteem.

It is crucial to start mastering fundamental skills as early as possible so that they become ingrained in us. This makes it easier to apply them in our day-to-day life. Unfortunately, what schools and colleges teach us about these skills is of little help as it is not programmed properly. No curriculum puts enough emphasis on these aspects. Schools that provide platforms for developing these skills directly or indirectly term such activities as extracurricular activities. Many times, the intent of these activities is not focused on the development of fundamental skills. Parents are also unaware of how these activities will help them in the future. Parents often force their children to participate in such programs without much thought. Stressed out, parents focus on academic results but forget their role in imparting these fundamental attributes. Also, they may not realize that when a child is compelled to do something they don't enjoy, it can harm their self-image if they do not perform well compared to their peers.

A child's self-image may be impacted due to several reasons. For example, the child may compare themself to others, developing an inferiority complex. He/she may be judged for not being able to speak well, not having good etiquette, being unable to present themselves to the group, not having attractive looks, bullying or harassment of any sort by peers or other groups, not scoring well in exams, not able to do well in other activities, negative assessment by teachers and more. They impact the child's self-image negatively, and the child may carry this image for their entire life. Once a person develops a negative self-image, it won't be easy to acquire the practical skills of life and move forward. Later in our lives, we realize that progressing further after a certain point becomes difficult.

We realize that individuals who progress fast in their careers and acclaim high positions have a different kind of stimulus inside them, which many do not possess. This stimulus of positivity comes from their positive surrounding environment or an innate focused mind, working towards clear objectives and goals. Even if you are talented but lack this stimulus, you may not achieve the same level of success. Here, A question, “Are these qualities innate, or can they be developed?” Much research has been done to suggest that these qualities can very well be developed in an individual. If one puts his heart into the transformation process. Training the mind in the correct manner is the key.

Our education system merely follows a process of selecting and rejecting individuals on a set parameter. This system brings out students who have a good understanding of the curriculum laid by the education board, ultimately to fetch a degree and get a job. The arena of success and happiness is secured for those who inherently possess these practical life skills or are lucky to be in a progressive environment and learn from it.

Every student has the right to learn important life skills, regardless of academic achievements. This includes those who may not have pursued higher education.

This book is not a plain, vanilla knowledge discourse. It provides clear insights and guidance on the main ingredients required to build a happy and successful life and the process of acquiring them.

Even if you pass the best professional courses, without fundamental and practical skills, you won't be able to lead a happy and successful life. Period.

"Success and happiness come from a strong culture based on life fundamentals, achieved through mind control."

Exercise:

1. What are the two halves of bringing up a successful career?

____

____

____

2. How can the self-image of a child be affected during schooling?

____

____

____

3. What do you understand by the term ‘success is a culture’?

____

____

____

Chapter 6
The Dream Life: An Alternative

There is an alternative to the present way of living. Why be under so much stress and be average.......

Exploring human behaviour reveals critical insights into the factors that drive happiness and fulfilment. Years of observation demonstrate clear patterns in how people live, what consistently brings them joy or sorrow, and the dynamic nature of these emotions as they evolve. Understanding these elements is essential to grasping the complexities of the human experience.

Personal problems and the unending quest to get material things hugely affect young minds and even the elderly. Without the right knowledge, striving for a happy life leads us nowhere, trapping us in a vicious cycle of manipulation. This pushes us further away from the ultimate goal of happiness. Our experiences and observations make us acquire a complex behaviour pattern that gives us less fulfilment. Further, degrading societal values only adds more to this stressful life. Despite increased convenience in our daily lives, desperation and stress have increased.

The prevalent antidote to this overwhelming situation is taking a break and going on a vacation. But that, too, is only limited to a few days a year.

I've observed the pain and struggle of people trying to overcome their challenges. During the journey, I interacted with people of several kinds and from different walks of life.

Each had their way of dealing with their life situations. While some were flexible in finding and trying new approaches to deal with their problems, most were relatively rigid in their ways, even if their behaviour caused them pain. They could not think beyond the boundary they had set in their minds.

My curiosity led me to read some religious scriptures; they provide a time-tested, proven way to lead a happy and successful life. I also read some books and analysed the lives of successful and content individuals. I studied the ethos of successful companies like Apple, Microsoft, GM, and others. I realized these people and companies have deep-rooted human values, and a well-defined process has guided them to a hugely rewarding business.

The distinction between an average company and a great company lies in how they treat human values. While average companies consider these values and required behaviours as added advantages for running their organization, great companies have these values deeply ingrained in their culture, thereby transcending these values to each employee.

We must understand the practical problems and the life skills required to lead a successful life.

Although we know what constitutes a happy life, we never delve deep to understand the necessary attributes to lead a happy life. In today's world, people generally bypass these attributes in favour of training programs to earn money. The tendency to take a shortcut route has easily manipulated the human race by several kinds of allures. These traps are laid in every step of our journey. Without proper evaluation, a person moves towards such allures and feels deceived or frustrated later. For instance, buying a product or service at a huge discount without verifying the quality of the product or service, or doing a course or a degree based on glamorous projections, relying on dubious online reviews.

The desperation to secure their lives quickly is the cause of misery for most Individuals.

Raaj Sinha

Some people develop practical skills for professional use but forget to apply them in everyday life, believing they are only for career advancement. This limited use of their abilities can lead to a stressful life overall, as the principles of interacting with others remain consistent in all areas.

Conversely, some possess a solid understanding of the spiritual world but struggle to incorporate that understanding into their professional and practical lives. They often keep their spiritual lives separate from their careers, leading to compromises in their professional behaviour that conflict with their spiritual beliefs. Navigating two worlds with differing philosophies can contribute to stress in their daily lives.

Therefore, choosing your career wisely is important because you spend most of your time with your office colleagues. Your job should align with your life philosophy and fundamental values. The framework for success presented in this book is built on a foundation that may be seamlessly applied to all aspects of life, with your core values at the centre of it.

It's time to transform our approach to life. By changing how we think, plan, and act, we can transform ourselves into an unstoppable person who applies the fundamental principles in every aspect of their lives to gain maximum success and happiness.

The SMS Framework:

It's possible to live a life where you feel in control of most of the things that happen to you. You can choose a career that aligns with your inherent skills or a work that makes you happy. However, to achieve this, you must take yourself out of the present muddle and enter the SMS rings — 'The rings of transformation'.

The transformation rings comprise the inner ring; Self-image; the middle ring; Mindset and the outer ring; Skills.

The principle of transformation lies in changing our self-image.

Your self-image guides you to accomplish any task or goal. Every action you take to reach your goal is based on your self-image. Even the behaviour we display in our day-to-day lives reflects the self-image we have inside us.

When you prepare for your career, the goal you set is important in determining what you will achieve.

Saina Nehwal, a former world no. 1 Badminton player, said that when she started playing Badminton at the age of 8, her coach told her that she would become world no.1. He wrote that on her racquet. Though she always focused on the next tournament that she had to play, this goal, subconsciously built in her mind, kept telling her to have no limits and chase all the targets with full dedication and determination.

A high self-image can convey a confident and self-assured presence in a demanding situation. Therefore, it is imperative to transform our self-image to achieve our imagined life.

However, your present mindset may not allow you to undergo a self-image transformation journey. Therefore, first, a mindset change is required.

Our mindset governs our thoughts. If we want to progress, we must expand our thinking horizon. New progressive thoughts have to replace our previous beliefs. Our thinking patterns have to change. We must leave our self-created prison, get out of our comfort zone and embrace a fuller life of abundance. The progressive mindset is the beginning of transforming you into a person of high self-image.

People with a high self-image can control their thoughts and channel them in the right direction. Additionally, they need a few additional skills specifically required to guide them in different and difficult situations to become successful in their chosen field.

Framework Diagram ...... [Fig 1]

Framework Diagram

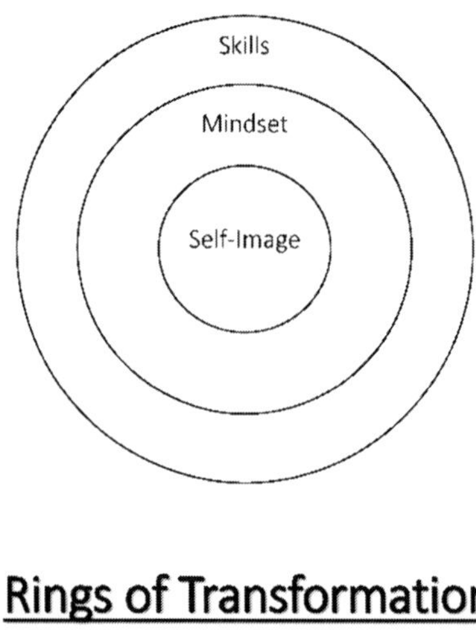

Rings of Transformation

PS:

As you delve into each chapter, carefully jot down all the necessary steps to transform and gradually bring them into your life. Observe and record the changes in your daily journal. Remember that the mindset you develop will drive the changes within you, enabling you to adopt the necessary attitudes and skills to achieve your goals. Take the time to revisit the chapters multiple times. Dedicate yourself to practising all the steps outlined and consistently maintain your efforts. Approach your work with determination as if your life hinges on it!

MINDSET

Chapter 7
The Formation of Mindset

"We cannot become what we want by remaining what we are."

"Mindset is Everything"

Our mindset is the sum of our beliefs, attitudes, and assumptions that influence how we perceive and interpret the world around us. It is shaped by our past experiences, knowledge, and exposure to different ideas and perceptions. Our mindset acts as a lens through which we view the world. It influences our thoughts, feelings, and behaviours.

Our current mindset is shaped by various impressions accumulated throughout our lives. These impressions are formed by observing our surroundings, learning from our parents and teachers, discussing with peers and friends, and so on. Whatever the mind perceives as correct while gathering knowledge or information from our surroundings contributes to the formation of our mindset. Unless our mind is wired differently and is willing to explore on its own, it will reflect the ecosystem we have lived or are living in.

The society we live in

Every living creature on earth has the natural inclination to establish and strive to accomplish its objectives. This innate ability is ingrained from an early age, often acquired through observation of parental figures and the surrounding environment. Individuals also develop the capacity to set and attain goals, experiencing a sense of fulfilment upon reaching their objectives. Subsequently, they proceed to establish new targets, perpetuating this cycle throughout their lives. In most instances, these goals and objectives are directly linked to the survival and well-being of the organism.

Unlike other species that are limited by their genetic code for survival, humans possess exceptional qualities that allow them not only to survive but also to thrive on this planet. Through ingenuity and resourcefulness, humans have found ways to make life easier and to ensure their continued flourishing.

However, human needs have become an ever-expanding zone of desires. While our primary focus remains on ensuring our survival, our aspirations extend far beyond mere existence. In fact, we now regard certain material possessions, such as owning a home, a vehicle, and various household gadgets, as indispensable for a secure and fulfilling life. We have established specific standards for attaining material wealth and other tangible assets, which we equate with achieving success in life.

This is because, over time, our brains have developed immensely, giving us countless ways to serve human needs and wants, giving us myriad options to earn a living and live a better life. However, this has led to a new problem: deciding which option or path to take can be difficult with so many options. We are almost spoiled for choice!

Today, there are hundreds of different ways of doing the same job, and each is subdivided into niche and micro-niche areas, thus offering thousands of opportunities. But today, most people are stuck in doing something they do not like. In reality, if you ask someone about job opportunities, they talk about the scarcity of opportunities in the job market. This happens mainly because we do not look beyond the kind of job prevalent in our community. We have to look beyond our boundaries for available opportunities. Therefore, we need to expand our context.

We limit ourselves with our thoughts to do only a few things. Our goals and aspirations are decided more or less by the boundaries set in our minds, subconsciously influenced by the community we live in.

Once we become aware of this fact, we will explore more opportunities, not just around us but beyond our community and land, and innovate new ways to serve our community. For example, one primary requirement is having food at work or at any outside location. This requirement can be fulfilled by:

Opening a food counter outside the workplace, if the requirement is high. However, number of persons ordering the food is less and the locations are spread out, a vehicle will drop the food off at the locations. It can also be done using an online food delivery application on the mobile.

Other ways to provide food based on business proposition would be to negotiate with the job-providing company to open a stall or canteen inside the premises. Providing homemade food at the office to people who are inclined towards homely food, Express delivery through drones to customers who value time more than money, serving hot or cold food as per requirement, food served with stylish dish plates and cutlery, Innovate food package, catering small party requirements instantly at the desired location, required drinks served with food, serving food at a location along with basic furniture, if required, food to elderly or sick served in the manner necessary, fulfilling before and after food handwash requirement, providing fruits, salads, and mouth fresheners, food for trekking/hiking, and food for fasting There is no limit to thinking.

Exercise:

1. Why is our thinking limited by the community we live in?

   ____

   ____

   ____

2. How was your vision limited by the community you lived in? Elaborate.

   ____

   ____

   ____

3. Find one primary requirement of the community and list five different ways of serving the requirement.

   ____

   ____

   ____

The squeezed-up society

Most of the population takes great pride in being labelled as middle class, and many strive to attain this status. However, it's important to acknowledge that this group is often the most oppressed. They are frequently subject to manipulation and endure significant hardships. Many individuals in this class experience a stark disparity between their aspirations and the harsh realities of their daily lives.

After investing sixteen years in education and obtaining a professional degree, many individuals face uncertainty and financial challenges. Despite the significant costs associated with education and training, most professionals in India secure jobs with monthly salaries ranging from 50000 to 80000 rupees (equivalent to 700 to 1000 US dollars). This income level is often insufficient to afford a comfortable lifestyle in major cities. As a result, many households rely on dual incomes, with both partners working to make ends meet amidst rising inflation and high taxes. The limited pay raises fail to keep pace with the increasing cost of living, affecting not only those with lower incomes but also making the upper middle class vulnerable, especially during economic downturns.

The issue at hand revolves around mindset rather than income. Most individuals have adopted a scarcity mindset, prioritising an easy life over facing risky challenges. Many openly admit they are not equipped to tackle bigger challenges and proudly proclaim they do not need to. They often believe that their education or skills make them worthy of a job that allows them to earn a decent living. As a result, they confine themselves to a narrow field in which they can earn, and the thought of venturing beyond this comfort zone instils fear in them. This mindset limits their ability to confront and overcome challenging situations, hindering their natural growth. Our inherent instinct to protect our boundaries and avoid difficulties has, in fact, weakened our thought processes. This behaviour prevents us from exploring new opportunities and fosters contentment with our current circumstances. Driven by fear and lack of confidence, these individuals constantly seek shortcuts or easier paths to achieve their goals. This often leads them to traps laid by manipulative advertisements and promotions.

This rigid mindset often persists even if someone attains substantial wealth. However, with a scarcity mindset, they may struggle to maintain that level of wealth and experience long-term happiness, ultimately leading to an average life.

One cannot lead a truly fulfilling life without a progressive mindset.

Duty bound by nature to hustle

While generally middle-class hustles, I used to believe that hustling was unnecessary in life and that things could be managed smoothly without extra effort. It seemed logical that if there were easier ways to make money, why should I choose the uncertain and challenging path? However, I eventually came to understand that this perspective was flawed. I realized that it's essential to exert the right amount of effort in the proper manner to achieve goals.

But hustling without a clear objective or goal is like running around a tree; you end up getting almost nothing significant. Therefore, align your hustle with your dreams and plans.

If our prime objective is to be happy, then we need to align our hustle with our goals.

Raaj Sinha

By nature, we are born to lead an active life to achieve our desires and set targets. We strive to give our best effort to attain what we desire daily. Avoiding life's challenges is like quitting on life and setting selfish boundaries to protect yourself from risks. This is not natural. Whenever any living being, including humans, starts to believe that their life has become risk-free. Conversely, they become more vulnerable to life's challenges. This gives rise to more stress. The person feels low on purpose, even though they exercise, eat healthily and try to keep fit. The energy and the life force will be missing, and they will feel like nothing exciting is happening.

For service professionals, regular employment provides a sense of purpose and engagement. Following a structured daily routine gives a feeling of accomplishment by the end of the day. However, individuals may experience a void upon retirement as they miss regular work's fulfilment and structure. Moreover, if they feel they haven't pursued their passions or missed opportunities, it can lead to a sense of emptiness and a decline in overall well-being. To maintain a high quality of life, retirees must find new sources of engagement or set meaningful objectives for themselves.

I remember witnessing this first-hand with my father. During his career in a government organization, his energy seemed boundless. He took the initiative in new projects, trained new employees, cultivated a sense of community among the staff, organized various cultural events and film screenings, conducted competitions, and supported the children. His quest to provide a better life for the young generation was unending. Despite all this, he had the enthusiasm and vitality to meet the needs of our large family. He always reflected a positive and energetic attitude.

After three to four years into retirement, I noticed a sense of unfulfillment in him. It seemed he had personal aspirations and dreams that had gone unfulfilled, and coming to terms with this realization was proving difficult for him. Throughout his life, he had received recognition from others for his numerous accomplishments, but this success left him with little time to pursue his personal goals. It appeared that life had passed him by while he was focused on the challenges of raising a large family and excelling in a demanding career. He often spoke of his desire to live a peaceful retired life in his own home and to have his car. While he did build a house, it may not have been the dream life he had envisioned.

After retiring, many individuals pursue various activities to stay active and engaged. However, often, these activities are simply extensions of their previous work responsibilities. But it can only keep the person happy if the job he has done in the past also kept him truly happy. Otherwise, it is just a drag. Engaging in activities that align with our values, goals, aspirations and fundamental attitudes is important. We will see this in later chapters.

Maintaining a positive outlook on life is essential in tapping into the abundance around us. Embracing an optimistic mindset, similar to the ever-pulsating energy of the Sun, allows for nurturing our life force. Consistently exuding energy, joy, love, friendliness, and cooperation can help cultivate a positive rapport with the world. Integrating vitality into our daily lives allows us to live authentically and connect with others naturally. Those aged should dream and plan according to their age and capacity to achieve their objectives or fulfil their desires. Have an objective that will give you a sense of purpose.

You should not just work for a living but also live for a better life around you. As it is said,

Not just add years to your life, but add life to years!

Exercise:

1. Why hustling is essential?

___

___

___

2. What do we learn by looking at the sun?

___

___

___

3. How do we avoid disappointment later in our lives?

___

___

___

Chapter 8
Be Accountable

A praiseworthy person walks the path of glory and failure with the same grace and humility. They never complain.

Every day, there are several things that you may feel have happened to you because of your thoughts and actions, while there may be several other happenings on which you had no control. Take this mundane activity. You rise up early, perform daily rituals and get ready for the office. Your breakfast is ready. You had your breakfast on time. You sit in your car and start driving it. Until now, all the activities have happened because of your thinking, planning, or acting. Further, while driving through the main road, you got stuck in a traffic jam. You reached your office late. A new urgent assignment came to you, disrupting your daily tasks. All this, you may think, is something you are not responsible for or is not a result of your thoughts or actions.

However, a successful person will have a different take on it. He believes

"Nothing happens to you; you make things happen for yourself."

Raaj Sinha

Success is not merely a product of efforts and random chance or sheer luck; instead, it emerges from a deliberate sequence of actions taken at the right moments. Some of these actions stem directly from our efforts, while others may rely on the contributions of those around us. However, we must still take ownership of the outcomes linked to these external factors, recognizing that our influence plays a critical role in their execution.

It's essential to assess the contributions we can make to ensure these necessary actions are carried out effectively. Moreover, if circumstances prevent the optimal execution of these plans, we should be prepared with alternative strategies, such as Plan B or Plan C, to adapt and navigate any obstacles that may arise. This proactive approach enhances our chances of success and reinforces our commitment to taking responsibility for our journey.

Individuals who refuse to take responsibility for the circumstances do not take much action and are generally unhappy in life. Their mentality ultimately becomes that of a victim. They tend to blame circumstances, events or people for something that has happened or has not happened in their life. As a result, they never achieve real success and remain a victim. The mediocre mindset is rooted in scarcity. They complain about everything - circumstances, no funds, surroundings, administration, etc. They say things like, "Why is this happening to me?" or "Why is God so unfair to me?" or “I do not have enough money to pursue this.”

Individuals who attribute their failures to external factors often find themselves trapped in a cycle of unfulfilled aspirations. They remain at the mercy of their circumstances, which ultimately stifles their potential for true success. In practical terms, life's journey rarely unfolds in the way we might wish; achieving meaningful goals demands personal initiative and responsibility. This principle holds whether one is pursuing individual milestones or navigating the complexities of a business venture. Every endeavour can be likened to a project, where the onus of reaching our objectives lies squarely on our shoulders. Embracing this accountability is essential for transformation and growth.

When managing a project, taking ownership of delays or quality issues is essential rather than assigning blame to others. Taking a case of procuring a critical material from a vendor. Before giving a purchase order, we assess their financial stability and production capabilities to ensure they can deliver the specified quality and quantity within the agreed timeline. To make a well-informed decision, one should also evaluate the vendor's previous track record for timely deliveries and their current commitments.

In addition to these factors, compliance with legal requirements and considerations regarding indemnity and insurance are essential. However, this initial assessment is just the starting point. Once a vendor meets these qualifications, they must provide a detailed production schedule with specific milestones.

Quality inspections are conducted at each stage of the production process. Upon completion of manufacturing, a factory test is carried out in the presence of the purchaser to verify performance standards. After the purchaser's approval, the materials are relocated to the site, where they undergo further testing under actual site conditions to ensure proper functionality alongside other systems and processes. In the project management process, we maintain a rigorous follow-up at each stage to ensure completion within the established timeline. If any delays arise, we provide necessary support to the vendor to address the issues. In the unlikely event of a vendor defaulting on the timeline, we proactively seek alternative suppliers to prevent significant project delays. This approach emphasizes the importance of nurturing strong relationships with multiple suppliers and other agencies, which ultimately benefits the industry in various ways.

The management understands that they are responsible for any delays, and blaming suppliers or other agencies won't help since such delays can negatively impact their industry's performance.

Similarly, to achieve our career and life goals, we must put in the same level of effort and take accountability at each step of the journey to ensure the success of our personal endeavours.

For the earlier instance of getting stuck in a traffic jam, a person focused on their goal will leave for the office early to avoid the peak traffic. Arriving early gives them time to plan their day, prioritise their tasks, and prepare for any urgent assignments that may come as a surprise. This planning helps them stay steady and focused even when faced with unexpected challenges. You would agree that it is nothing big. It is just a shift in mindset.

If you are a teenager or a young adult feeling overwhelmed, hopeless, or unmotivated, know that you are not alone. It's easy to feel like life is not going your way, and you have no control over it. However, this is the perfect time to awaken and take charge of your life. Don't let external factors or negative experiences dictate your future. Instead, stay resilient and focused. Recognise that you have the power within you to overcome any obstacle and find a solution to every problem. Believe in yourself and take the first step towards a fulfilling life. Remember that you can achieve great things and that your potential is limitless. You may be putting effort in an incorrect direction or in a less effective manner.

Let us understand this: say you have your exams tomorrow, and electricity in your area has gone off due to some issue. And it remains so throughout the night. Now, will you not read under a candle, even if it's challenging to do so on a hot summer day?

When you assume responsibility for your situation, you become more proactive and come up with solutions to move forward. Otherwise, you become passive, keep blaming the circumstances and remain a crybaby.

Believe that every outcome directly results from what we are thinking or doing. A person is the originator, the source of everything in his life. This attitude will give the person the power to take responsibility and control the situation.

I used to attribute my failures and lack of progress to external circumstances during childhood. I felt that the situation was beyond my control and that I couldn't consistently improve myself. I often felt powerless and believed that my present state was determined by fate. I also believed that if I worked too hard to change my fate, it would only bring more pain. Unfortunately, this kind of thinking is common among people who feel stuck in life and don't take decisive action to improve their situation.

In hindsight, when I look at my mother's life journey, I see a lot that can be taken as inspiration. I haven't seen her in a helpless situation. Even in the most challenging circumstances, she will fight and come out of it without complaining. This behaviour is inherent to her, and I haven't seen her struggle when faced with challenges.

She got paralysed in 2003. Half of her body was numb. Her limbs on one side were not moving at all. Doctors advised her to an exercise regime, but they were not hopeful of recovery. However, she followed her daily routine of exercise, diet, medicine and, most importantly, the determination to fight and become fit. She could recover completely in 45 days, with no signs of paralysis ever again.

Again, when she was living alone, she fell unconscious in the kitchen garden. During that time, I was at a remote location doing a project. When she regained consciousness, she called my wife on her mobile phone and said that she was feeling dizzy and that getting up from the floor was difficult. (Luckily, she fell with the mobile phone in her hand.) My wife realized that it was an emergency. She flew to my hometown, picked her up and got her admitted to a hospital. The doctor diagnosed that her heart was not functioning properly. She was operated upon to get a heart pacemaker. But during that crucial period of more than 24 hours, she kept her fighting spirit to survive that emergency. Deep inside her, she has a belief in overcoming any challenge. Now, she has some other medical conditions related to her lungs. She has COPD, with only 30 per cent of the lungs functional. I have never seen her missing a single medicine intake as prescribed by the doctor in the last fifteen years.

She gets this ability from the way she has lived her life. I have seen how she has brought up her five children in the best possible manner with minimal resources. She never complained of falling short of anything. She always brought out the best that was possible for her at that time.

She has always encouraged me to go for big things in life. She never let her energy dip and fought through several odds to bring us up. In all the problems the family encountered, she had this one weapon to fight it out – A determined mind to step up to the challenge and come up with some solution through her hard work and efficient management of resources. During my childhood days and even beyond that, whenever I got the opportunity to be with her, I didn't see her wake up late. By the time we woke up, a pressure cooker was whistling in the kitchen. She probably wakes up early and does all her exercises. She never let her physical ailments come in between her willingness to thrive in challenging situations. A few years back, when my father fell ill and was suffering from dementia, she took care of him like the best caregiver. She had never had any desire for herself but all for the family. Though she had gone through several such challenges, I have never found her complaining. She is an inspiration to me!

In the corporate world, every employee has a set of responsibilities that they must fulfil. However, what sets apart a truly exceptional employee is their ability to perform their role in a way that positively impacts the overall functioning of their department. By completing tasks on time and to the required standard, employees demonstrate their dedication and commitment to their jobs. An employee's sincerity can also be reflected by their interest in the department's overall performance and their willingness to contribute to its improvement. Helping colleagues with their work is a great way to show this sincerity, and everyone appreciates it. When a new or more demanding assignment comes to the department, those who show sincerity and dedication will be the first to come to the manager's mind.

Whether you are in a leadership position or not, a basic attribute of leadership quality is owning accountability for any activity in your area of work or the company you are working with.

If you are an entrepreneur or intend to become one, you have no option but to be accountable for everything. You have to plan for all challenges, whether economy-related, competition-related, personnel-related or policy-related. Therefore, take control and be accountable for everything in your life. Blaming a situation or person doesn't help in any way.

No blaming. No bitching. No moaning.

Remember, if we are taking credit for our success, we have to take responsibility when things don't go as planned. It is the sign of a leader. When you work with this mindset, you already operate like an authority. Your words are valued.

It will take you to the level where you start taking control of everything that helps you succeed.

Exercise:

1. What is accountability?

___

___

___

2. How does accountability improve your chance of success in your work?

___

___

___

3. How does self-image drive you towards being more accountable? How do you become a more reliable person in your company?

___

___

___

Chapter 9
The Right Approach

We discussed how the surroundings influence our mindset and limit our progress.

We will explore further and find the correct way to approach life for happiness and growth.

A non-progressive mindset is sometimes called a 'middle-class mentality' or a 'mediocre mindset.' It's important to know that this isn't about financial status. You can be wealthy and still have a mediocre mindset.

A progressive mindset is essential for success in professional and personal endeavours. Even with natural talent or acquired skills, reaching and maintaining a higher level of growth is unattainable without a mindset that is receptive to change and progress. Regrettably, numerous instances of affluent individuals ultimately lived mediocre or disadvantaged lives due to their lack of progressive thinking. Notable examples include Bernie Madoff, Patricia Kluge, Vijay Mallya, Elizabeth Holmes, Boris Becker, and many others. Acknowledging how having a mediocre mentality can hold us back from growing and succeeding is crucial. Sushil Kumar, a 22-year-old brilliant boy from a poor background, won five crore rupees (three-quarters of a million USD) in a television show and lost it all by poor investing and frivolous spending as per the advice of the people around him.

The gap between our aspirations and our actions has become increasingly evident, highlighting a significant disconnect that we can no longer ignore. This realization encompasses the understanding that our daily choices and behaviours do not truly reflect our inner desires and goals. It has prompted us to recognize that we have not been fully aligned with our authentic selves, leading to frustration and disconnection.

It's not entirely our fault, as we didn't have enough exposure, and our visibility beyond our ecosystem was limited. We had no idea of how to get to our dreams. Our limited exposure led to limited outcomes, and it's possible that subconsciously, we were solely focused on ensuring our survival, navigating with excessive caution.

The realization to seek greater harmony between what we wish to achieve and the steps we take to reach it prompts us to reflect on our childhood and how experiences shaped our approach to life as we grew up.

A child's dreams are limitless; they naturally aim high. However, instead of nurturing these dreams, we often focus solely on ensuring their future, which can lead to greater disappointment, as we have discussed. In this approach, security becomes our primary goal in life.

As we grow older, we tend to abandon our dreams during adolescence and shift our focus toward securing our future. At this point, many of us begin to give up on our aspirations and make compromises.

It's important to recognize that if we continue to approach challenges with the same mindset that led us to struggle, how can we possibly expect our children to break free from those limitations? To truly help them achieve their dreams, we need to inspire them to think beyond our own experiences and embrace new possibilities.

Consider the potential outcomes if individuals had grown up without negative influences, similar to the mindset of a child who possesses untainted perspectives. By studying these traits, we may discover their advantages for personal growth and well-being. Let's examine some of them.

A child's mindset

As children, we focused on discovering and cultivating activities that resonated deeply with our passions and interests. This process involved exploring our innate talents and skills, allowing us to better understand our natural abilities and what we genuinely enjoy. By doing so, we aimed to align our pursuits with our intrinsic motivations, ultimately fostering a more fulfilling and engaging experience in everything we do.

A mind free from fear can explore new experiences and opportunities. It involves being open to stepping out of your comfort zone, trying unfamiliar activities, and welcoming the unknown with curiosity and excitement. This attitude encourages personal growth, enhances creativity, and fosters resilience, allowing you to discover new passions and build deeper connections with the world where you want to go. By cultivating a willingness to explore, you can unlock a wealth of experiences that enrich your life and broaden your perspectives.

Having complete confidence in our abilities and the wisdom our teachers imparted. This belief not only empowers us to pursue our goals but also fosters a strong relationship with those who guide us on our journey. Embracing this trust helps us to overcome challenges and encourages a collaborative spirit in learning and growth.

No matter the challenges we face or the obstacles that arise, we must continue to push forward and persevere. It is through our consistent efforts and dedication that we will ultimately discover something new and valuable. Let us remain committed to our journey of learning and growth, embracing every opportunity to expand our knowledge and skills.

Learning from our failures is crucial for personal and professional growth. It's essential to analyze setbacks without letting them discourage us. By understanding what went wrong, we can make informed adjustments and improve our future efforts.

Never judging others' acts or words, enjoying one's own experiences and taking things objectively. No biased opinion for anyone.

Authentic love and pure expressions of care are characterized by simplicity. They exist without the entanglement of jealousy, resentment, or internal conflicts. Such feelings create a nurturing atmosphere that encourages open communication.

Summarizing:

1. Direct our efforts to learn things we love to do intrinsically, i.e. your inherent capabilities.
2. Not being fearful about exploring new things.
3. Having complete faith in ourselves and those who teach us.
4. Come what may, keep striving till we learn a new thing.
5. Maintain unwavering focus on the goal until you achieve it.
6. Learning from our failures and not getting perturbed by them.

7. We should not judge others' acts or, for that matter, our own.
8. Genuine love and empathy, devoid of complex emotions and internal conflicts.

We will discuss it in the self-image section of this book.

Risk and Reward

The bigger the impact you would like to make through your chosen field and the bolder the purpose is— the greater risks you will have to take. This means there is a greater chance of failing.

Clearly, there is a conflict between predictability and making an impact, between safety and living your purpose in life.

Let’s go through a typical family discussion.

Mom and Dad have scrimped for several years to provide their children with a good education so their children can get a leg up on life. When the daughter goes to college, she decides to pursue a course or degree in drama, art history, mass media, or fashion design. A fight ensues.

Parents: But how will you earn a living as a painting artist or through creative writing, philosophy, literature, poetry, etc.? How many ads do you see for such hiring? Remember, we are middle class; we do not have much money to experiment with all these things.

Daughter: But Mom, this is what I am passionate about. I don’t want to live my whole life serving wealthy people, making them even richer and letting my passion die inside me.

Parents: We understand your passion. We only suggest that you consider a backup plan, not because we doubt your talent, but because we want to ensure your secure future. Imagine if you could combine your love for painting with a career in finance. You could become a chartered accountant, a profession in which you can excel, and still pursue painting as a side passion. This way, you could have the best of both worlds: professional stability and personal fulfilment.

Daughter: You will never understand me. There are bigger and more meaningful things to do in life than just thinking about job security. You never like me to be happy!

Parents who have worked so hard for their kids' bright future have a limited outlook on the future, forcing them to make decisions that turn their children into average achievers. While you may have chosen safety over the risk of exploring new things in life, in the process, you pushed the child on a not-so-liked and difficult path without taking the complete future perspective into the picture.

This happens when we have limited options to explore the future and a need for a clear vision of how the future will shape up. When we cannot foresee the outcome of our efforts in the required detail, we may not be able to set ourselves on the correct path to success. And sometimes, even if we know the outcome, we do not know how to get there. Unfortunately, many people don't have the necessary exposure to plan effectively. They could only look within their limited environment for opportunities to pursue. Some tried to venture into unknown territories but left in between, as they didn't find those opportunities convincing enough. Having the right mindset is the key to manifesting our dreams.

In India, there is still a common trend among parents suggesting engineering as a backup plan for their children. However, this often leads to several students who lack interest in engineering pursuing it anyway, resulting in them becoming mediocre contributors to their field. This can lead to dissatisfaction and a waste of time and money. Ultimately, many of them may end up struggling to make ends meet. It is crucial to understand why you are pursuing a particular career path. What kind of success do you want to achieve, or how will it satisfy your inherent desires or skills? This is not just about career choices; it's about the quality of life and personal fulfilment.

60% of people feel emotionally detached from their jobs, and only 15% are passionate about them. This means they do not feel motivated every morning to go to work. We inflict such pain on ourselves only because we didn't plan well initially or we didn't have the right outlook.

Courtesy Job unhappiness is at a staggering all-time high CNBC.com.

Since we have talked about how risks in life influence our decisions at every step, let's delve deeper into this topic.

Success is not solely about personal gain; it mainly involves contributing to the well-being of others. An essential aspect of success is serving people. Helping and being helped by others is integral to a successful life's journey. To lead a fulfilling and meaningful life, making a positive difference in the lives of those around you or the community is essential.

Striving to positively impact people's lives often involves navigating various challenges and uncertainties. This endeavour can be particularly risky, as it may require you to engage directly with individuals through face-to-face interactions or by creating something meaningful within your community. Such engagements can lead to situations where you might face rejection or fail to receive the acknowledgement you hoped for despite your honest intentions and hard work.

The deeper your desire to support, help or entertain others through your professional endeavours, the greater the likelihood that you will encounter obstacles along the way. Whether you pursue a career as a teacher, where nurturing students' growth is paramount; as an artist, where your creations are exposed to subjective interpretation; or as an engineer or doctor, responsible for critical decisions impacting lives, each role carries its unique risks and rewards. Yet, these risks are often accompanied by the profound fulfilment that comes from making a difference in the lives of others and contributing to the greater good.

Our society is constantly developing and evolving because somebody takes the risk of initiating change. Of course, they learn the necessary skills and take calculated risks. No risk means no exploration, no experimentation, and therefore, no advancement of society regarding better service or product.

It's important to explore ways to impact people's lives positively. It doesn't need to be big in dimension, but one has to be devoted to serving.

We need to understand that there is risk in everything we do. It is through managing the risk that thousands of businesses thrive. You must identify risks in your chosen field and learn how to handle them. Your reward will be commensurate to the bigger risk you handle. Running away from risks is no solution to the problems we face.

Let us understand this. Don't you take risks when you board an aeroplane? Wherein, in case of an accident, the risk for loss of life is maximum. Yet, you board it, why? When you were on the flight for the first time, you might have felt scared, but only briefly. You subconsciously gained confidence because you have heard or know that a relatively small number of accidents have happened compared to the number of flights flown. Had the rate of accidents been higher, you would have been afraid to board a plane, even if the tickets were cheap!

In terms of safety and reliability, aeroplane travel is currently the most dependable and quickest mode of transportation. This can be attributed to the significant advances in aircraft design. Despite these technical advancements, the pilot remains the key person. Pilots must be brave, remain calm under pressure, have grit, have a good presence of mind, have high learning agility, and attention to detail. Therefore, they command high respect and remuneration in the industry. If you compare the remuneration of flight crew, ground maintenance staff, and others, a pilot's salary is higher when divided by the hours worked. This is simply because a pilot has a high risk of flying every passenger safely to their destination. Now, think about the owner of the aviation business. He/she is the one who took the risk of starting the business by putting in the money, time, and effort and, today, facilitates thousands of passengers every day to reach their destination safely and comfortably, providing income to hundreds of staff and their family members. He is impacting the lives of thousands every day. Therefore, his share of profit is the highest. He is also accountable for the risk borne by staff members and the business loss, if any. Therefore, the greater the impact, the greater the risk and the higher the reward.

How to handle risks:

Take a few cases from our daily lives to get some perspective on risk and reward.

We are often afraid of public speaking but not of driving a car or riding a bike. Despite knowing that the risk of getting injured while riding a vehicle is higher than while giving a speech, most people would still choose to drive. This is largely influenced by mindset and perception. The key to taking risks is to evaluate them properly.

Putting a new product on your shop shelf to attract customers. One aspect may be that it only gathers dust there, and the campaign for selling the product does not take off. However, the other side could be that adding this new product significantly improves your revenue. But to improve your business, you must go for newer products.

Should I ask my boss for a promotion or a pay hike? The consequences of asking are that you get the boss's nod or you don't, and the consequences of not asking are that you may not get the hike or promotion. Realize that consequences like embarrassment or hurting your pride are rubbish that will only hold you back in life.

The explanation fits when a boy has to propose to a girl on a date.

If you look at risk this way- Asking the girl is the ONLY way to get a good result.

You can make the risk matrices for any decision.

One will have to get comfortable with being uncomfortable. It pushes you out of your comfort zone to do things that you dream of. The psychology of being uncomfortable is related to one's mindset and self-image. Once you acquire a high self-image, please return to this chapter and go through it.

A wise advice would be to prepare or assess ourselves before we ask someone for a favour.

The first step is understanding ourselves— strengths and weaknesses. Then, work on priority areas, which are your high-risk areas, i.e., those that may act against your desired outcome. Work upon those and strengthen them. This prepares us to take on more challenging situations.

If you plan to set up a business, make a proposal plan. Analyse business prospects and profitability. Identify the critical areas and do a risk analysis to understand areas of high consequence and the probability of an unwarranted event that may impact business negatively. Focus on providing required safety measures to control or overcome such eventualities. After listing out the required safety measures against the risks, perform another systematic round of risk analysis to see if there are major changes to the initial plan. Once all the risks are listed along with actionable, rewrite your business plan. This way, one can conceptualise a better business proposal.

The focus of a personal development plan is to overhaul our minds and make them work efficiently towards the defined objectives. To make the mind work efficiently, we must build a strong self-image. A strong self-image requires a strong character, which will be tested under various challenging circumstances.

This means striving to become more authentic in thinking, acting, and behaving. Character defines us. Therefore, your character, combined with the required skills, will prepare you to become efficient and handle more ups and downs without strain.

We must break free from the traditional non-progressive mindset, discover our true selves, and set goals accordingly. Pursuing something that aligns with your true self is always a safer and more effective way to move forward. For successful career planning, it's important to follow the right process. Similar to technological advancements in aeroplane building, we must gather sufficient data. Guiding principles are developed based on the gathered data. Various pieces of information come together to build a knowledge base to find the correct way of doing things. This is how you gain wisdom in any field or in life in general.

Being part of a group with shared goals can help you stay focused. A mentor or guru can also offer the guidance and support you need to navigate real-life challenges and work towards achieving your goals.

"The formula for success is no secret. It has been tried, tested, and proven several times. First, work on your inner engineering to change your old mindset and develop the right one. Then, establish a positive self-image, find your purpose in life, engage your creative thinking, set your goals, and become a 'go-getter'.

Some examples of how a non-progressive mindset is differentiated from a progressive mindset:

Mediocre mindset:

Some popular myths about goals in life.

- Set moderate and realistic goals [Realistic means what they already know].
- Do not take undue risks; focus on securing a safe job.
- Do not venture into new things. Go for goals that are tried and tested by hundreds of people (people in their community)
- Very few job opportunities.

Common approach is

- Not open and flexible to change.
- Blame circumstance or society for failures.
- Seeking shortcuts to secure themselves.
- Good health is important to avoid costly hospital bills.
- Money is dirty and can only be earned through illicit ways.
- Knowledge and money cannot go together, contradicting each other.
- Save money for a better future for children.
- Live with a scarcity mindset: Sacrificing health, family, and time for profit or earning.
- Relationships are obligations to be fulfilled. Limit it to avoid losing focus on life goals.
- Less inclination to learn from other cultures and societies, believing our culture is far superior and sufficient.
- Intelligence is a repertoire of the few gifted ones.

Contrary to this,

A Progressive Mindset:

- Set high goals and keep reviewing them every day without compromising them.
- Take massive action to achieve your goals
- Venture into the unknown, solve new problems or find more straightforward ways to solve a problem. (Nothing is less risky, if you calculate your risks and get the right knowledge. Keep moving step by step to reach your goal.)
- Takes complete accountability for their failures and never blames anyone.

- Fair understanding of the fundamental principles of life and applying them practically in life.
- Open to adopting new things in life puts them on a constant quest to acquire sound knowledge.
- Celebrating success and learning from failures. Therefore, acknowledging both with equal grace and humility. Failures are a major part of a success story.
- Start with whatever money is available. Don't wait for piling money.
- Seize the opportunity at the earliest. Opportunities come and go fast.
- Knows how to leverage work to maximise profit.
- Set goals to serve a larger section of society. The more people are impacted, the bigger the success.
- Choose a profession to solve people's problems. Work hard and learn the rules of the game. Money is a by-product; if you serve well, it will automatically come.
- Maintain physical and mental health for efficient performance. Make it an essential part of the routine.
- Invest in children's future by building their character and allowing them to explore and learn to take risks.
- Relationships are the greatest asset. Building good relations and networks is essential.
- Grow money by investing wisely for better returns.
- Explore scriptures, read books, and visit places to learn about different cultures. Be open to adopting the goodness of other societies and cultures.
- Intelligence can grow and blossom with effort.

One should consider these points when setting their goals in life.

Chapter 10
The Power of Belief

In the beginning, we discussed faith, which stems from our belief system. Anything we want in life should conform to our belief system; otherwise, we do not provide the necessary impetus to pursue it. It would be a waste of time to think, plan, or act on something we do not have faith in. That is why we started by becoming hollow and empty, allowing us to build a new system of belief and faith.

"Believing in yourself" is a widely recognized idea vital in determining our actions and accomplishments. Many of us are familiar with this concept, but how often do we stop to consider its significance deeply? Why is it that we struggle to believe in ourselves when it comes to pursuing significant goals in life? Why do our dreams remain unfulfilled due to a lack of action? Why do we often struggle to sustain our efforts, whether it's a project, habit, or any other endeavour? These essential questions warrant thoughtful reflection, especially when motivational stories and pep talks fail to translate into consistent action.

Our belief system is deeply ingrained within us and can be challenging to change. It is formed based on the opinions and influences we receive during our upbringing from friends, family, teachers, and other people in our lives. This process occurs as we transition from childhood to adulthood. Our beliefs are rooted in our subconscious and are shaped by the self-image we hold of ourselves. This self-image is located at the core of our subconscious mind.

Our self-image plays a crucial role in our ability to succeed. If we see ourselves as successful, we will approach every situation with positivity, calmness, and focus. This positive outlook will motivate us to achieve more in life, and we will be open to opportunities to gain knowledge and serve others. We will be driven to plan and work towards our desires.

Instead, if we see ourselves as victims, we become negative and critical and complain frequently. We surround ourselves with negativity, blind to see the good things happening around us. Our energy levels are low, and we cannot find opportunities to contribute to society. We miss out on opportunities coming our way.

A person with a low self-image lacks the courage to pursue their desires, as they do not believe they can achieve them. Therefore, it is essential to cultivate a better and bolder self-image.

It's a well-known fact that children who have low self-esteem tend to struggle with their academics and face difficulties in practical life. Parents and teachers should encourage children to make good attempts and praise them whenever they do so instead of comparing their efforts with others. This will help children think well of themselves and never feel inferior to their peers. It's important to note that we should recognize and appreciate a good effort rather than just the final output.

Also, children should not be forced to participate in all kinds of extracurricular activities. Instead, activities should be chosen based on their interests and preferences. We must be mindful of our efforts to help children and young adults build better self-esteem and confidence to pursue their dreams and not force them into areas where they do not have interests.

Nobody is born with the idea of being inferior or superior. It comes only by comparison. You tag yourself as inferior when you compare yourself with someone who has excelled in a particular field. When somebody scores higher than you, despite your hard work, or when others act, sing, or play sports. Similarly, when others are perceived as beautiful or intelligent, you may begin to believe you are less than them. This subconsciously sows an inferiority feeling in your mind.

The fact is that every individual is unique, and everybody has some innate talent. Instead of realizing this, we compare ourselves with others. This may lead to tagging ourselves as superior or inferior. The problem here is that it does not remain for a particular thing. Instead, it portrays us as negative individuals. This psychology in the mind builds up slowly and gets conformance every time you make such a comparison.

This feeling of failure or inferiority can be reversed when you think you can do many things. You may possess some innate qualities or have acquired some through sheer determination and hard work. You have to believe in yourself as a winner.

Recalling past success, even a small one, can instil a winning feeling that paves the way to success. Start giving these positive signals of being successful to your mind. If you have done it once, you can do it consistently. Remember, you didn't do well in between because you didn't think you would succeed in that work.

This is particularly important for children, who need tasks they can complete successfully. The task should not necessarily be related to the course but to various things of interest to them, which they are happy to do. Tasks should be within the child's capability so that they can complete them and feel motivated.

On completion, the child will get a winning feeling of completing the task well. This way, we build success patterns in their brain. They become forthcoming to take on new projects and successfully complete them.

I observe that most of the tasks given to the kids are difficult to do, as they do not have enough practice. Parents are fully involved in completing their child's work. Subconsciously, the feeling of accomplishment is deprived.

For adults, you may recall any instance from the past when you got recognition for a job well done, no matter how small it might seem. Relive such an instance and bring out the feeling of accomplishment or success you experienced. Live the moment again to instil the feeling of a winner inside you.

However, if you cannot think of any such instance, you can also bring out the feeling of a winner by taking small projects and completing them successfully, just like the children. Such projects can be as simple as forming a new habit of arranging your room in a way that places things in a convenient location, and at the same time, the arrangement gives a feeling of a settled or sorted mind. Practise breathing exercises regularly or start a morning or evening walk. Completing these tasks will give you a sense of achievement and help build confidence. Do it with consistency. Celebrating small successes and remembering them when you face challenges helps. Trusting yourself and your abilities is crucial in building confidence and resilience to face new challenges. This also helps you identify your strengths and weaknesses and become more open to change for the better.

It's important to remember that everyone makes mistakes in life. It is a part of the learning process. When you recognize your mistakes, it's a win for you. Rather than abhorring them, cherish them, as they will remind you of the lessons you've learned.

One of my colleagues at my workplace used to be very depressed as his efforts were not recognised. His seniors would make fun of him for his clumsiness at work (filling presentations with unnecessary details). He lost confidence, and his presenting skills deteriorated further. His interest dipped. Gradually, his attitude became that of a rebellion, as he was not cooperating and complying with the requirements. One day, a new and different assignment was given to him. Though this assignment was unrelated to his field of experience, he took it with interest. It was about managing employee training and maintaining a database of training activities. He worked hard and presented a sincere and impressive report for this assignment. He was acknowledged by his seniors, which reignited his motivation. We could observe marked improvement in his presentation. His rise in confidence led to significant improvement in his core competency of piping engineering, and he soon became a grade-A employee.

Realizing the sense that “I am a person of value” has a great effect on an individual's output.

Remaining unfazed by the task at hand is an excellent quality for an individual. Our resilient and confident nature is a great tool that propels us through adversities. So, the question is how to regain that quality. It comes through the power of belief in oneself—belief in the power of the almighty and in the power of infinite intelligence guiding us.

The power that creates magic every moment, it has driven us to achieve remarkable feats: we can fly, circle the earth in hours, instantaneously connect with anyone worldwide, condense huge libraries into a small device, travel to the moon, explore stars, build skyscrapers from the earth materials. The race to transform these into new things has just begun. "It is possible to create anything we can imagine, provided we put our full faith and emotions into it." By taking one small step at a time. This power resides within each of us. After birth, it is this power that makes us walk after a struggle for several months, eat on our own, learn to understand and talk, and many more.

Our beliefs are also formed out of values we carry inside. These values inspire behaviour and actions. Therefore, our actions result from the values we carry within ourselves. We must look into our values to see if they produce average results. If yes, it's time to change our beliefs.

As one's belief changes, the intensity of the positive signals the brain transmits changes, significantly impacting outcomes. This is essential in our journey towards success.

Once you believe you are successful, your behaviour and actions will also reflect this. It is said that once you begin your journey, your beliefs change with experience. But this is a hard and tiring way to learn. Rather, when you operate with a higher self-image and a winning mindset, you remove obstacles and clear your path towards success. You achieve your goals faster.

Allow me to tell you a small instance from my college days: After the end-of-semester exams, we enjoyed the train journey home, singing songs, sharing food, and cracking jokes. On one of our journeys, a few elderly men in our compartment watched us having fun. One of them asked, "What do you do?" One of us replied, "We are engineering students." After we got introduced, the gentleman asked, "You all are doing engineering from a not-so-renowned college; will you be able to get a good job?" My friend replied with all humility and calmness, "I am not seeking a degree to do a job for someone; I aspire to give jobs. If you have anyone who needs a job, you can ask him to contact me after a year or two." There was complete silence for a moment. This context never entered in the minds of those gentlemen. We usually do not think beyond the frame we have built through our exposures. That friend of mine, from a humble middle-class background, runs a 500+ crore (Seventy million dollar) business in the Delhi-NCR region.

Self-belief helps you create a new self-image without limitations. It works on your subconscious mind, and your actions and behaviour are governed accordingly. This happens because you change the core of your thinking process through self-belief. If we are convinced that nothing is impossible, we awaken the magical power within us. Here's another powerful incident to substantiate this.

The Miracle man

Morris Goodman, an American, was a college dropout with no clear direction in life.

One day, his eyes fell on a book called "Think and Grow Rich" by Napolean Hill. Curious, he started reading the book and learned about the subconscious mind. He started working on expanding his subconscious mind. As he descended into the depths of his subconscious mind, he could talk with his mind at ease, giving and receiving directions within to lead his life. After some time, he started his own business, and within a few years, he became a successful businessman.

But this story does not end here. When Morris Goodman became a successful businessman, he bought his aeroplane, got a pilot's license and started flying it. One day, while flying, his engine suddenly failed. He tried emergency landing but was unable to do it. His plane crashed and hit the ground so severely that it exploded. Goodman was in such a bad state that he could not even breathe.

He was taken to the hospital, where doctors found his entire body paralyzed. He was not even able to breathe properly, nor could he speak. He could only blink his eyes. His spinal cord was completely broken, and he could only breathe through machines.

After a few days of treatment, the doctors informed his family that Goodman would never be able to breathe on his own.

Even though Goodman could not speak or move, he could hear. When he heard the doctor's words, he completely refused to accept them in his mind, as he was aware of the power of the subconscious mind.

Then he told himself that doctors cannot decide my future, cannot determine what I can and can't do!

He decided in his mind that after precisely three months from today, he would get up from this bed himself and go out of this hospital. He always kept this positive thought in his mind and worked on it. Surprisingly, just three months later, Goodman got up from his bed and walked out of the hospital alone. This miracle baffled everyone. None of the doctors could understand this possibility.

And today, everyone knows Morris Goodman as a Miracle Man. He is an American motivational speaker who travels worldwide, telling his story.

You get the power of belief in yourself when you have a firm 'winning feeling' inside. This winning feeling doesn't come until you have a clear picture of 'how' you will get it. Once you have figured it out, practice it consistently until you become better at it. The result will automatically follow.

In one of our leadership development sessions at a beautiful resort near Mumbai, we played a game designed to foster belief and confidence. Twenty of us were paired in ten groups each. One person in the group was blindfolded, and the other had to encourage their partner to throw a tennis ball into a bucket at a distance of 15 feet. The other partner only encouraged, "You have great abilities, and you can surely put the ball in that bucket." I lost my sense of direction when I was blindfolded and rotated two to three rounds. I felt it was impossible to throw the ball, as I could see nothing but darkness. Where is the bucket? Where to throw the ball? I thought this to be a crappy game. My partner started encouraging me, expressing his belief in my abilities. His encouragement made me recall similar games I played as a child. I got the confidence as I started visualising the bucket in my mind, managed to put 7 out of 10 balls in the bucket and won the game. It was the power of belief. Even though I could see nothing, I knew I could do it, which changed the outcome.

The 'power of belief' has been the life force since life sprouted on this planet. Through this, we evolve continuously in all spheres of life. The power of belief shapes and moves the world.

Reconstructing a new belief system is through the transformation of one's self-image.

- Start firmly believing that you are meant to do great things.
- You are not here to make compromises but to break all barriers to achieve and live your dream life.
- Learning a new skill is just as preparing a new delicacy.
- Nothing is difficult. It is all in mind. Build a strong mentality to overcome any challenges. Practice a lot till you win over your fear.
- Every human is different but equally capable of reaching its own destinations. Set your destinations, and do not venture into paths not meant for you.
- Do not take your failures negatively. Get lessons from it.

Feeling Blessed

Do this small exercise to feel and believe that the almighty force is guiding you all the time:

Sit or lie down comfortably and close your eyes.

Relax, take a few deep breaths, loosen your body and keep your spine erect.

After you feel relaxed, focus on your breath gently. Feel the incoming and outgoing breath through your nostrils. *Imagine that every exhale takes away your worries, and every inhale fills you with new energy.*

Keep breathing until you feel light from inside.

- Now visualize a ray of golden light coming towards you from a distance from the skies. [15 seconds]

- Slowly, the light is getting brighter and brighter. [15 seconds]
- Observe the warmth as the light gradually engulfs your whole body. [15 seconds]
- The light warmth builds up the ravel care that your soul needs. [Feel the moment]
- You feel safe and protected [Feel the moment]
- A new energy is getting unlocked from within. Feel it move through the veins to all parts of your body. [15 seconds]
- You feel connected to the divine energy. You are charged with a new gush of confidence.
- Deep inside, you bow down to the almighty with gratitude. You feel God's light flowing through your body. Now, the energy is creating excellent propositions for your life. You are the divine's choice to create magic in your way.
- Feel this protection all the time. Keep doing it every day for the first 45 days, and it will become a regular practice.

Exercise

1. How is our belief system formed?

____

____

____

2. How can you win over fear about something?

____

____

____

3. What steps will you apply to convert a negative belief about the self into a positive one?

____

____

____

4. How does feeling blessed help you in your work?

____

____

____

SELF-IMAGE

Chapter 11
Self-Image: The limiting factor

Self-image is not just about how people think of themselves, but also about the subconscious image of self in their mind. A strong and positive self-image acts like a control unit that guides a person's actions towards achieving their goals. When goals are achieved, it further validates the self-image, reinforcing confidence and self-esteem.

An individual's success is greatly influenced by their self-image. Unfortunately, many people's self-image is negatively impacted during their early years and throughout their education. A person's self-image is largely shaped by the validation they receive from others. Superficial changes such as having a high-paying job or position or trying different tactics to grow will not necessarily lead to a happier life and greater success. Changing our perspective and beliefs about ourselves is essential to achieving success and fulfilment.

Focusing on self-image is pivotal in self-development because our confidence and fear of doing a job also stem from it. A high self-image that is aligned with your goals is a sure way to achieve success in life. It is imperative to comprehend our current self-image and the reasons behind the need to modify our behaviour and attitude to adopt a successful self-image. This change isn't just a transformation but rather a complete rebirth of an individual!

The Inner Voice

If you aspire to lead a good life and strongly desire to fulfil your dreams, you must align your mind, body and soul in one direction. But it is easier said than done. Most of us struggle with desire on one side and our subconscious mind on the other. Your subconscious mind tells you- "This is difficult", "You have never done this", or "It is not for you". Even before you can start your transformation journey, you give up as your inner mind has given you a negative validation, or many still pursue it only to get disappointed in the end.

We also see that people start on their new journey to realise their dreams, but when they face challenges of several kinds, they abandon their journey midway. This is because of the self-image they carry. It also comes as an inner voice, which is not always strong. It tells us how capable we are to perform the job.

Where does this inner voice come from? What is its origin?

On your journey to attain true success, it is of foremost importance that you understand yourself with earnestness. Your desire to achieve your dreams should be fervent.

You need to identify your true personality. People unconsciously resist looking inside them simply because they fear discovering who they are. They live their entire life portraying either a made-up or fearful image. Most of the time, a person doesn't know exactly what kind of personality they have.

A false negative belief about oneself can become deeply ingrained due to interactions with society and the opinions of others, leading to a wrong self-image.

The Validation from others

We must understand that every individual was a gifted soul when he came to this planet— a pure soul. Let us understand a child's journey from his birth. When a child is born, they already have a vague self-image built in. Their mind is structured to absorb everything from their surroundings. For every act, they seek validation. They observe that their acts are being noted with much interest and applauded. When they utter the first word, the family cheers. Likewise, achieving every milestone brings immense joy to the family.

As children mature and engage with the world more fully, they often become more expressive in their interactions with others. In response to this development, parents, family members, and teachers play a crucial role in providing guidance and lessons intended to support the child's growth and prepare them for future challenges.

Typically, each child is expected to navigate a standardized educational curriculum that outlines a specific path for academic achievement. This curriculum is designed to impart essential skills and knowledge that are deemed important for all learners. However, it's important to note that this one-size-fits-all approach doesn't consider the unique variations in each child's learning style, cognitive patterns, personal interests, or inclinations. Consequently, while every child is exposed to the same educational framework, there may be missed opportunities to tailor teaching methods for providing learning experiences more suited to individual strengths and preferences, potentially limiting their engagement and enthusiasm for learning.

For instance, if a child discovers a passion for a particular arts subject, such as fashion design or fine arts, after completing the 8th standard, they may have to wait before they can officially select subjects that align with their interests. During this interim period, students must complete a set of core subjects that may not resonate with them or spark their enthusiasm.

This obligatory curriculum can include subjects that feel unrelated to their aspirations, such as a deep and varied understanding of mathematics, science, or literature, which might lead to frustration and disengagement. As a result, the necessity of engaging with these less appealing subjects can negatively impact the child's self-esteem and self-image. They may begin to doubt their abilities or feel disheartened, particularly if their passions lie in creative fields that are not prioritized within the educational framework.

A student in my school excelled in physics, particularly in electronics. At a very young age he was making models that were being acclaimed across international platforms. His technical advice on choosing the right technology for a high-power television transmission tower in the neighbouring district was highly praised, even though he was only in the 8th grade. However, he struggled in several other subjects, including some science subjects. Unfortunately, this system often causes great distress to prodigious minds who develop an interest in a particular subject at a young age. Therefore, many abandon their education at some point in their student career. This situation highlights the importance of allowing students to explore their interests more freely while also recognizing the value of a well-rounded education.

The majority of achievers in different fields and Nobel laureates are not those who score well in all their school subjects. Rather, they show deep interest in the subject of liking and keep working on it to produce path-breaking results that have changed how we live our lives. Then what is the present education system producing? This has been the topic of debate for a long time.

The present education system has pros and cons; one definite positive is that it provides millions with opportunities to lead better lives and contribute to a progressive world.

Let us go through different cases of students' journey after schooling.

Case 1:

Many students in the current education system step away from their true interests to pursue various professional courses for a few years. After working in these fields for some time, many realize that it may be too late to follow their inherent talents. They may become singers, preachers, businessmen, advocates, financial analysts, social workers, or politicians.

Considering a working life of about 50 years—starting at age 16 and remaining active until 66—many spend over 15 years pursuing careers that may not align with their passions.

Some argue that these years are not wasted, as they acquire valuable skills. However, one must ask: how relevant are those skills to their chosen career? Take the examples of successful industrialists, such as Warren Buffet, Steve Jobs, Dhirubhai Ambani, and Elon Musk. Numerous examples in the field of art and sports. They began working on their careers early, and this early focus significantly benefited them later.

Case 2:

This is about students who pursue a path they never intended for themselves and lack the courage to change direction. These individuals often compromise and feel pressured to conform to workplace expectations, ultimately engaging in work they do not enjoy. Over time, they may accept their job, but in the process, their self-image begins to erode. Unconsciously, a traumatized self-image takes root. This transformation occurs gradually and subconsciously, leading many people to remain unaware of the changes within themselves. In my case, it took me around 20 years to recognize this.

Case 3:

Not all Individuals with strong intellect and aptitude may necessarily have the mindset to navigate, reproduce, and compete within the current education system. Evaluated by this rigid framework, their knowledge in various subjects may not resonate with them. Despite having excellent aptitude and intelligence, the system often overshadows them.

Consider a diverse group of professions: artists, columnists, reformists, administrators, advocates, salespeople, entrepreneurs, scientists, philosophers, sociologists, politicians, subject teachers, interior designers, graphic designers, chefs, guides, trainers, stylists, public relations experts, spokespersons, athletes, and even specialized engineers, among many others. If all these individuals are required to follow the same path previously discussed, they will likely not excel.

As they go through this process, their self-image can suffer significantly. Only a few possess the resilience to recover from this experience, while for many, their promising dreams come to a sudden halt.

Parents have seen this system from the beginning and know no alternate approach exists. Therefore, all our teachings and preaching to the child are aimed at excelling within this framework. We also evaluate them accordingly. However, if the child cannot meet our expectations, we internally start judging them. Society judges every child based on established norms. School is often the first place a child begins developing this complex.

Parents do not realize that they might not know everything the child needs for proper development, as every child is unique. However, they tend to become champions of child psychology and give guidance they think is best for the child. Parents' mature mind knows the hardships of life, and every thought is biased towards securing the child's future. Being short on knowledge to understand the complete perspective, parents stress achieving the immediate goal. The child feels the pressure from a young age, leading to a declined self-image.

As time passes, a particular self-image becomes more vivid and resides in the core of a person's subconscious. The mind automatically rejects anything that does not conform to this self-image, which becomes firmer by receiving similar signals over time. A person's actions and behaviour are always in alignment with his self-image.

Dr Maxwell Maltz, in his all-time classic *Psycho-Cybernetics, explains:*

"Each one of us lives with a self-image that our conscious mind may not be aware of." This self-image is the perception that conforms to the kind of person we are. It is built up with our own beliefs, which are formed by our past experiences of successes and failures, accolades and humiliations, predominantly experienced during childhood and adolescence. This belief is so firm that we never question it. A student who thinks he is a failure will have his report card to justify his thinking. This continues every time until he gives up, quits the process and tags himself as a failure. This means that the student will never be able to grasp the subject. While going through the project, he already had a feeling that the subject was difficult. The mind will be fearful and compressed, not allowing it to absorb new concepts. Unless the mind is comfortable with the subject, taking or retaining the knowledge inside will be difficult. A person can never act beyond his / her self-image, even if he tries very hard and in whatever way.

Unfortunately, only a few can maintain or develop a high self-image. When they enter the practical world, many develop a low self-image, which becomes one of the biggest hindrances in their journey to success.

Thus, your surroundings played a significant role in creating barriers in your path to progress. These mental barriers are formed by others' validation and your acceptance, impacting your future negatively. A person who does not accept negative validations may still be able to maintain and balance their positive self-image.

Exercise:

1. How does validation from others affect the self-image?

____

____

____

2. How do the limitations of self-image affect our growth?

____

____

____

3. How can you disallow the negative validations to affect you?

____

____

____

Chapter 12
Self-image and Self-Esteem

Understanding the Difference between Self-image and Self-Esteem.

Many people often mistake self-image for self-esteem, but they are two separate concepts. Self-image refers to the subconscious boundaries that limit our actions and decisions throughout our lives. At the same time, self-esteem is more related to the value of oneself and the moral values we earn and maintain through our actions and behaviour. A high self-image can lead to high self-respect and self-esteem, but the opposite may not necessarily be true.

For example, a person may feel that they are not good at communication and, therefore, feel uncomfortable expressing themselves, whether written or verbal. This notion might stem from poor marks or validations during schooling years. This limitation solidifies into a mental boundary, guiding their decisions and limiting their choices. Now, they would live their entire life with this limitation. Their mind will subconsciously guide them to do things within this limitation. For example, since communication is an essential tool for leadership, they might avoid roles that require leading others. This is the limitation of the person's self-image.

However, self-esteem is the respect a person has earned for themselves for their work or deeds. A person with high self-esteem can carry this self-esteem into their work, driving them to produce results to the best of their abilities. Also, if situations threaten their self-esteem, they might withdraw to protect it.

Therefore, within the boundaries of one's self-image, one can excel and earn self-pride or self-esteem.

When someone says, "I am confident I will be able to do this," or conversely, they may say, "It's not my cup of tea," this outcome is derived by comparing the job at hand with the self-image one has in its core. Self-image is a fundamental aspect of our lives, as it guides us in taking action and making decisions. Therefore, regardless of our strong or weak self-image, we tend to be protective and resist new challenges. When faced with challenges, we hesitate, fearing failure, which could harm our self-esteem. Therefore, we are protective of the boundaries of our self-image.

Chapter 13
The Beginning of Image Makeover

For a star to be born, there is one thing that must happen: the gaseous nebula must collapse. So, collapse, crumble. This is not your destruction. This is rebirth.

-n.t.

This is not your heart breaking, my dear; this is your heart hatching. Breaking the shell of who you once were. This is your rebirth.

@Axiom.attic

Our lord has written the promise of resurrection not in books alone but in every leaf in springtime.

Martin Luther

The Triggers to Transformation

If you want to accomplish more in life than you currently do, it's essential to broaden or rebuild your self-image. Fortunately, it is feasible to transform your self-image at any stage of life, as confirmed by several scientific studies. By grasping this idea early in your career, you can reduce the time spent in agony and misery while significantly enhancing your chances of achieving genuine success. This realization can be a game-changer in terms of personal growth and development.

Many individuals have achieved great success after changing their self-image and self-discovery, even in the latter part of their lives.

Take the case of Mahatma Gandhi, the 'Father of the Nation' for India, who led the successful campaign for India's independence. In his early years, he chose to become a lawyer. However, after completing his studies, he could not practice his profession successfully as he still carried his childhood shyness and self-withdrawal. Psychologically, he was unable to cross-examine his witness. That led him to take a mediocre job of working for a meagre salary with an advocate.

But after facing racial discrimination in South Africa, his inner self emerged. He refused to budge against the British administrators and led a few movements against the oppressive rule. He decided that he would never fail to express himself. He devised a new way of resenting oppressive British rule by fasting, non-cooperation and non-violence. All his limitations were exposed when he stepped into the public domain for a social cause. These limitations were erased quickly as he accepted the job, which was different, big, and challenging, which revealed his strong character. His approach and complete belief in non-violence have created a mark on human civilization, a legacy still taught worldwide.

When individuals become aware of the reasons for their suppressed or unjustified state, they often experience a shift in their self-image. This shift occurs when they confront the situation directly and actively work to address it. Sometimes, changes in self-image happen when you switch careers, where previous validations may hold less significance.

Consider the case of those who were previously struggling in academics. When they get onto a different life skill job, such as sports, taking over a family business or pursuing work that aligns with their natural abilities and personality, they gain the confidence needed to become successful individuals. Entering a new environment erases a part of their old self-image since their previous negative validation is no longer relevant. They feel comfortable working, producing good results, and receiving positive feedback, which helps to create a new self-image. Sometimes, this may still reflect aspects of their old self-image, but this does not negatively impact the overall outcome.

Change at the opportune time

In many jobs, employees are frequently compared to their peers by their bosses. Sometimes, one may receive a good rating, while at other times, one may not be rated as highly. To cope with such situations, managers are required to explain the benefits of rating and its limitations. Ratings are just a limited assessment of your performance for the year and should never be used to berate a person personally or professionally.

When individuals consistently receive low ratings or feedback in their professional environments, it can create significant barriers to their advancement, impacting their careers and overall quality of life. This ongoing struggle with negative perceptions can lead to diminished self-esteem and a lack of motivation, making it challenging to pursue new opportunities or personal growth.

In such situations, it may be beneficial for individuals to reflect on their current work environment. Considering a company change or even a career path shift could provide a fresh start and open up new avenues for personal and professional development. By moving to a new setting, individuals can focus on rebuilding their self-image, emphasizing their fundamental strengths and practical skills rather than merely conforming to the expectations of their current roles or supervisors.

This approach encourages a more holistic view of self-improvement, one that is based on a deeper understanding of one's unique competencies and passions. Instead of becoming overly fixated on external validation, it is essential to cultivate an inner confidence that relies on one's abilities and growth potential. Embracing this mindset enhances one's professional trajectory and can lead to a more fulfilling and satisfying life.

Transforming oneself is a serious process, and understanding its mechanisms is essential. Unfortunately, many individuals fail to progress beyond a certain point. Transformation involves changing habits, behaviours, and overall character. However, people often struggle to integrate these changes into their lives. As many of us have experienced this: we start by joining a gym, practising meditation, enrolling in a skill-improvement course, and committing to becoming more disciplined and calmer. However, somewhere along the way, we tend to falter. The weight of change becomes too heavy to bear.

Have you ever wondered why this happens? Why do we struggle to keep up with the changes we set out to make?

The answer lies in our self-image. Remember, anything that is not in congruence with your self-image will be rejected. You feel the heat of transformation because you are rubbing against your self-image. It is subconsciously rejecting your new endeavour.

Adopting a new habit is not easy. Research has shown that only one in ten people succeed in changing their self-image by developing new habits. Most fail to maintain these new habits consistently. Our brains are wired to follow established patterns, and it takes significant effort to break them. We need to change those patterns and create new ones to make a lasting change.

Instead of forcing ourselves to adopt new habits, we should focus on understanding ourselves and building a new self-image. This approach makes the transformation process achievable and enjoyable. Working from the inside out can create real and lasting change in our actions and behaviour, ultimately producing the desired result.

Working the other way around is the miracle mantra!

Once we commit ourselves to this process, we begin to feel transformation as gratifying and start removing barriers holding us back. You can effectively go on to improve your inherent potential. You need to discover it.

First, envision the outcome of this process— what you will become—and then work through the required steps.

But visualising the person you aspire to become requires constructing a new self-image.

To unleash our true selves, we must remove all barriers created by false perceptions gathered from our early experiences and interactions.

I realized that I had several limitations built into my self-image.

Unable to be in good health

I always struggled with maintaining a healthy body. Frequent episodes of physical illness made it challenging to improve my health. I believed my weakness and frequent illness were due to my genes, making it impossible to achieve and maintain good health. This mindset made progress difficult despite trying to lead a healthy lifestyle. I ended up falling sick again and again, making me feel even more helpless and discouraged. I feared that if I pursued greater challenges in my career, and my body would not be able to handle them, I would end up right where I started. This fear prevented me from trying new things and taking bigger risks.

After much consideration, I decided to attend a week-long program aimed at helping people achieve happiness in their lives. The program had a truly profound impact on my life, completely shifting my perspective. I began practising meditation and breathing techniques, and as a result, I noticed a significant improvement in my strength and immune system. Over time, I became more adept at controlling my yoga postures and thoughts, and I could feel my inner voice transforming. As a result, I became more confident in myself and my abilities.

Book reading: A waste of time

I strongly believed that people should form their own philosophy based on their experiences rather than wasting time reading about others' life experiences. Also, I thought watching a movie is a better way to assimilate knowledge, as you could learn more in less than three hours than spending days reading a book.

However, this belief changed during my transformation journey. Reading books significantly impacted my mind more than watching movies or TV shows. This is because movie scenes change rapidly, making it difficult for our brains to analyse and retain the information. However, reading allows you to go at your own pace and reread sections to understand the content entirely. Reading books from different authors and backgrounds has taught me valuable life lessons and gained newer perspectives. This helped me broaden my understanding of the world and acquire wisdom to apply.

I developed love for reading books.

Exercise:

1. Why are we unable to acquire new habits?

___

___

___

2. What is the first step to take before getting into the transformation journey?

___

___

___

3. How does changing your environment or field of work transform your self-image?

___

___

___

4. What steps should you take to protect your self-image from getting affected?

___

___

___

Chapter 14
Understanding self-image

"It is not the mountain we conquer, but ourselves."

Sir Edmund Hillary

Achieving a higher self-image can bring unimaginable joy to your life. It can make all the difference between success and failure. When you have a positive self-image, you will start feeling better about yourself, and your perspective on life will change. You gain clarity in your imagination. Also, your goals change. Your thinking will broaden, and you'll be able to identify the right path to reach your goals and remain focused on your objectives. You'll know the purpose— 'why', which will become the driving force in all your endeavours.

The Self-Image Pattern [The hypothesis]

The concept of self-image and how it works has been explained in this section with the help of a hypothesis. It will help you to understand the concept in a better way and use it to visualize and develop your new self-image. Let's try to understand how our self-image functions and how it is affected by interactions with the outer world. A graphic representation of the hypothesis has been created to help with your imagination process of directing the right signals to the brain.

Functioning of the subconscious mind

Imagine our mind's memory store to be in the form of concentric circles. The innermost circle can be called the nucleus or core, and larger circles surround it as we move outward.

Thoughts arise when we listen, see, observe, or contemplate ideas. These thoughts travel in the form of electrical impulses in our brains. The strength of these impulses depends on the emotions associated with the thoughts or words.

Thoughts that are not properly formed or have lesser emotion attached to them generate weak signals and do not travel beyond the outermost circle. However, well-formed thought generates stronger signals and goes deeper into the concentric circles. These thoughts represent themselves in the form of a pattern. Also, the core or the nucleus of our subconscious mind stores permanent concepts in the form of images or patterns. If the pattern in the core and the signal pattern that has entered the concentric rings match, then the nuclei pull the new pattern into the core. This makes the core pattern bolder.

Other powerful emotional signals can also enter the concentric rings surrounding the core. Although their patterns may not align with the core pattern, they can still travel through the inner layers. These signals can complicate the core pattern by getting integrated into the existing pattern, creating blocks or barriers.

Thoughts that cannot reach the core are temporarily stored in concentric circles. Over time, these thoughts fade away or diminish. In contrast, the permanent thoughts held in the core shape our thinking and behaviour. These patterns reflect one's **self-image**.

The design inside the Nuclei can be either simple or complex. A simple design presents a vivid and clear pattern, while a complex design shows a less distinct pattern and depicts a more intricate self-image.

Signals can be received from external sources or from within the self without distinction. Acceptance or rejection of signal occurs at the outermost layer. If the signal is accepted, it moves to the inner layers; if rejected, it falls away at the surface. This process of acceptance and rejection usually happens subconsciously. When similar signals are accepted repeatedly, they make impressions, forming an element of the core structure or pattern. As discussed earlier, our mind creates a detailed picture of ourselves for comparison purposes with any new incoming thought or suggestion. This vivid image has clearly defined boundaries that dictate our capabilities and limitations. Once established, this self-image subconsciously influences our actions, behaviours, and decisions. Therefore, we are unable to do anything beyond the boundary of our self-image. We don't even realise the subconscious limitations built inside us.

Normally, when a child is born, their core base is simple and may lack clear patterns. Early in life, the core is still developing decision-making abilities and thus accepts almost all signals, thus forming the base of the core. This base is mostly positive as we always support, love and encourage the child to grow into a better person. Therefore, every child has a base of peace, love and care. As they grow, they receive positive and negative signals from friends, colleagues, peers, family, relatives, strangers, situations and circumstances that start forming impressions influencing the core pattern.

For reference purposes, signals congruent with the core base will be called positive, and opposites will be called negative.

Self-image evolves during different stages of a person's development. A well-defined core interacts effectively with received signals, whereas complex or weak cores produce ineffective responses.

Positive signals enhance the core pattern, making it bolder and creating a better self-image. A strong core has better thinking, intuition and decision-making abilities. Fig 3

However, repeated negative signals introduce barriers and patterns that hinder the positive pattern in the core, resulting in a complex pattern. Fig 4

Core patterns subconsciously influence action signals. There can be cases where the incoming signal somewhat matches the core, but in the absence of a strong core, these signals may remain in the outer layers and fade away.

<u>Definition:</u>

1. **Barriers [Negative emotional attachments]:** Limiting attitudes and beliefs results in low self-capability to take action.
2. **Complex pattern [Negative behaviour]:** No clarity of thought and purpose leads to Complex Behaviour and a lack of focused approach in life.

The slightly less complex pattern or more complex pattern, refer to figure 5, allows the formation of similar patterns in the layers formed around the core.

How the self-image works: Raaj's hypothesis on Self-image Patterns.

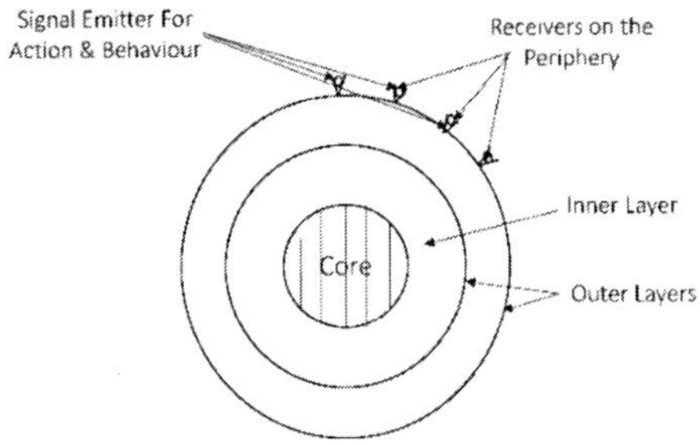

Diagram [Fig 2]

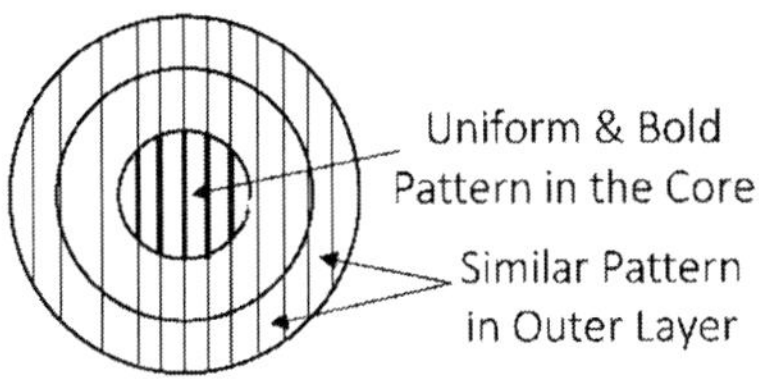

<u>**The pattern of a highly efficient Subconscious Mind**</u>

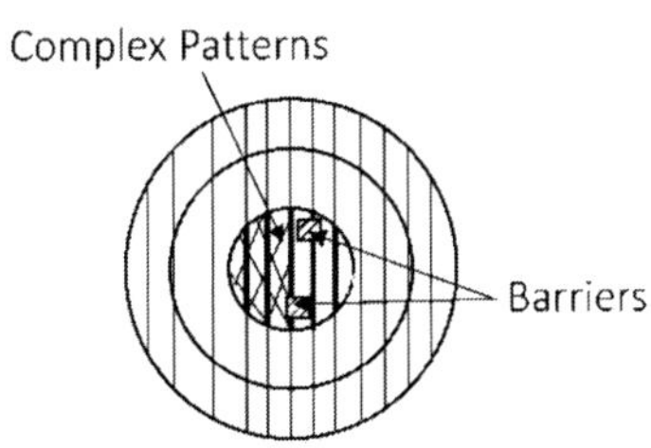

<u>**The pattern of a highly inefficient Subconscious Mind**</u>

[Middle][Fig 3] [Personality type A]

[Bottom][Fig 4] [Complex Personality]

Examples of Core Pattern Complexity

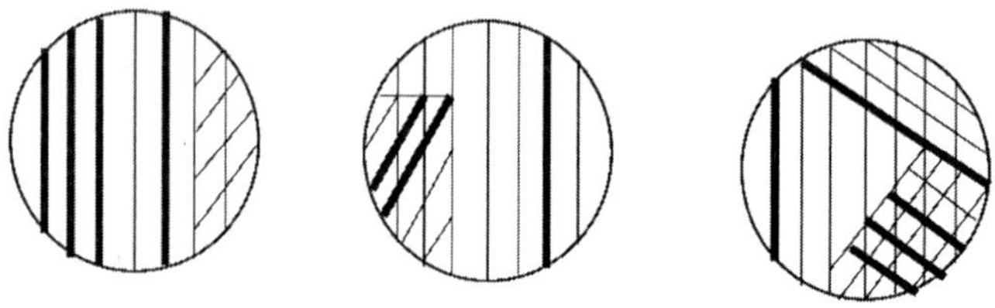

Slight Complexity   Medium Complexity   High Complexity

[Fig 5] [Personality type B, C, D]

- *Disclaimer:* Our Brain has several facets for receiving and storing information and a response mechanism. It is vast and beyond the scope of this book. The above representation is made for easy visualization of self-image and focused development of personality and goals.

Strong personalities often characterize individuals with a pure or less complex core. They embody unwavering principles and established habits, exhibiting high energy, efficiency, and output levels. Their subconscious thinking processes are fast and clear, enabling them to progress, grow, take calculated risks, and achieve greater objectives with relative ease. Such individuals tend to set and accomplish their goals more rapidly.

Conversely, individuals possessing a core with mixed or complex patterns may encounter challenges when attempting to act with the necessary intensity. The command signals generated by their core tend to be weak and fail to transmit effectively, resulting in indecision and a lack of clarity across various domains of their lives. These individuals often struggle to make prompt decisions and may have hesitance in navigating their life paths. Their propensity for risk-taking is diminished, leading to a general aversion to embracing challenges. Notably, most of the population presents with mixed or complex patterns.

Furthermore, individuals with complex core patterns may not display consistent behavioural traits. They may harbour biases against certain individuals, objects, or behaviours, and their interests may fluctuate significantly, often leading to abandoning previously favoured pursuits. Consequently, maintaining positive habits, behaviours, or actions can prove difficult for these individuals, resulting in challenges in establishing clear life goals.

The personality (A) type [Fig 3] represents a successful personality because its behaviour is consistent with its inner thought process.

- High energy and positivity
- Defined goals and objectives and focused direction.
- Clear and consistent thought process.
- Fast decision-making abilities
- No conflicting opinions and effective control over their thoughts.
- Healthy lifestyle and readiness to seize opportunities.
- Consistent thoughts and confidence
- Actions and behaviour aligned with their principles
- Strong leadership qualities.

Personality (B)(C)(D) [Fig 5]: Individuals with complex core do not transmit strong signals for actions and behaviour. They may set goals but soon sputter and stop taking action.

- Lack of clear direction
- Unable to form strong values and principles for their life.
- Display low energy and an inconsistent approach.
- Exhibiting conflicting opinions and reduced understanding of situations.
- Struggle with setting clear goals and seizing opportunities.
- Have inconsistent thoughts and lack confidence. They are inconsistent in their habits.

Exercise:

1. Why does a simple core pattern make a strong core?

___

___

___

2. How do impurities impair the efficient functioning of the subconscious mind?

___

___

___

3. What kind of personality does a complex core represent?

___

___

___

4. List down your limiting beliefs. Explain, in short, how they have hindered your growth.

___

___

___

5. List down your behaviours like procrastination, indecisiveness, etc. and explain how they stopped you from growing.

___

___

___

BUILDING SELF-IMAGE

Chapter 15
Self-Discovery: Self Awareness

Knowing our present core and its related action behaviour is necessary for transformation. This means we need to know how we handle different situations in life. What do we value? Do we have defined objectives to lead our lives? If yes, what are they?

When we can see ourselves clearly, we realise what has been holding us back, the areas that need to be prioritised for improving ourselves. In the process, we gain confidence and learn to express ourselves clearly. The confidence stems from the realisation that we can improve. We let go of our thoughts and behaviours holding us back and acquire the attributes required to build a better personality. Self-awareness is a practical skill that improves our emotional intelligence and other leadership qualities.

Whether you are a student or a professional, we all want lasting success. Understanding yourself is deeply valuable. We may have to look deep inside ourselves with thorough honesty.

To illustrate this, consider the following story.

Who am I?

A revered sage was returning to India after travelling the world. On his way, he stopped over in a small princely state.

When the king heard of his arrival, he immediately rushed to meet him, bowing at his feet and said, "Master, I have had an unresolved question for the last 20 years. I am unable to find an answer to it. Will you give me the answer?"

The sage replied, "I will, for sure. Today, you shall receive your answer."

The king continued, “Does God exist in reality? I only wish to meet him directly.”

The sage asked, "Do you want to meet him now or after a while?"

The king clarified, "Excuse me, but I don’t think you understood correctly. I am talking about the Supreme Father, the Supreme Soul, not a mere man named God.”

With a smile, the sage said, "I understand it, gentleman. I do the work of connecting people with God. Do you want to meet him now or wait? You've been eager for 20 years. Now the time has come, so meet him."

The king took a deep breath, gathered his courage and agreed.

The sage instructed, "Please, write your name and address on a small piece of paper so that I can convey your identity to God."

The king complied with the request, including his titles and personal introduction, and handed it to the sage. The sage replied, "Sir, everything you have written on this paper seems incorrect to me. Tell me, if your name were to change, would you also change? Would your consciousness, truth, knowledge, and personality change?"

The king answered, "No, a name is merely a label. I remain the same. So, the sage continued, "One thing is certain: the name is not your introduction because you do not change by changing it."

"Now tell me, if you lost your kingdom and become a poor citizen of the village, will that change who you are?"

The king replied, "No! Even without my wealth, I will remain the same as a poor citizen. My thoughts and my mind remain unchanged."

Then the sage remarked, "It is clear that the state is not your true self.

What about your age? It represents your body and the changes it goes through, not who you are?"

The sage concluded, "Your age doesn't define you.

Write down who you are, and I will inform God. If you can't identify yourself, how can I introduce you?"

The king admitted, " I don't know who I am. These are the only things I know about myself."

The sage said, "Then find out who you are. Once you discover your true self, you will realise knowing yourself, you also know God."

We often fail to explore ourselves deeply. If you ask anyone, "Do you know who you are? Whatever you pursue in life now, is that aligned with your true self? Mostly, the answer is, "Of course, I know who I am and what is good for me". He may even add, "Do you think I am a dud?"

Tasha Eurich, an organisational psychologist, and her team conducted ten separate investigations involving around 5,000 executives and a study of 800 research papers. They concluded that only 10–15% of people are truly self-aware.

We can enhance self-awareness by comparing our behaviour to our core values. Shelly Duval and Robert Wicklund explained in their Landmark Theory of Self-Awareness 1972, "When we focus on ourselves, we evaluate and compare our current behaviours to our internal values and standards." In other words, when you focus on yourself rather than your environment, you compare yourself with the standards of correctness, revealing your true self.

Here, becoming a sentry of our behaviour to understand mind reactivity is an excellent tool to have throughout the day. Just keep watching; don't make any effort to stop it. This means keeping a watchful eye on our thoughts and emotions without trying to stop them. By observing our mental patterns and reactions, we can gain insight into our subconscious and better understand our mind.

As an individual, you will feel a sense of pride or dissatisfaction depending on how well your behaviour aligns with your standards of correctness. If you're dissatisfied, you might make changes to your behaviour or change your present environment to match your standards better. For instance, if you value compassion but realise that your behaviour has often slipped away from being compassionate, hurting others. Then you would strongly like to change your attitude towards others. Similarly, if you value truthfulness, but your present job doesn't value that, then you may have to change your work environment. You might seek to change the role that better suits your creative aspirations.

As discussed earlier, negative behaviour is often the result of negative patterns built into us. These patterns can hinder our growth, happiness, and peace.

We can progressively eliminate these barriers and patterns and channel our energy constructively by identifying them. We must analyse the barriers in our core. Some of these result from observing people around us and our surroundings. However, the major ones are accepting opinions and judgements given by others in the past. We must release these attachments back to the source from where the negative energy has got into us so we can channel our energy to build ourselves efficiently. We will go through the process of releasing negative barriers in the next chapter.

Now, we will analyse the negative patterns and their corresponding behavioural responses. Then, we will undergo the necessary process of releasing those patterns from our core.

A behavioural control illustration:

Ravi, a manager in a multinational firm, became angry when his colleague's presentation missed out on an important achievement of the department in overcoming a long, unresolved issue. Ravi's reaction— overreacting and demeaning his colleague— reflects a tendency to magnify issues. He needs to explore why he reacts this way. He needs to realise that such behaviour is not in line with the values he carries inside, as whenever he sees a calm and balanced person, he develops respect for that person. On contemplation, he might find that his anger stems from past experiences with authoritative issues he experienced from his seniors. Recognizing these connections can help Ravi manage his reaction and improve his leadership.

If Ravi is unable to see the connection between his present behaviour and past experience, his control over his present behaviour will be limited.

Another example:

Satya is the head of sales for his organization. During a department's progress review meeting, he noticed a dip in sales numbers. Without analysing the situation, he immediately blamed his team for not putting in enough effort. However, he should have considered that the dip in sales might be due to a better and more competitive product launched by their competitor. Satya's past experiences have influenced his way of thinking, and he tends to see things through a filter. For example, when he was a child, he struggled with mathematics, and his father would scold him for not putting in enough effort. Nobody had the patience to make him understand the concepts. He could not score well in exams. This experience left a scar, and he has faced several similar situations where his views or limitations were not given due attention. His present reactivity is linked to his past experiences.

By understanding the connection between his past experiences and present behaviour, Satya can learn to see situations from a broader perspective to avoid making such mistakes, rectify himself and become a better leader.

Similarly, on the relationship front, most behavioural issues are caused by the negative patterns we carry within. Negative behavioural traits pull us away from accomplishing our goals in the true sense. They deter us from being a good personality.

Self-induced Barriers

We also discussed that some of us form barriers within ourselves by observing and comparing with others.

Examples:

Many of us struggle with self-doubt and negative thoughts like," I'm not good enough" or "I don't deserve happiness." These often stem from personal failures and the belief that the world is cruel and unkind. For example, I have not done well on several occasions. I am unworthy and undeserving of good things in life. Instances in my life clearly tell me that this is a mean world. The incidents that have happened in my life or by observing incidents that happened with others, I can tell that people are selfish and cruel. I have been ditched; people are untrustworthy. There's hopelessness all around; only a few rich people are capitalizing on the situation.

We might develop an insecurity complex about our appearances or abilities, leading us to question our worth and potential. For example, I am not beautiful or smart. I am not presentable enough. I lack the etiquette required for being in a decent society. People don't like me. I have done bad things, and I deserve to suffer. There's something wrong with me. I try to study, but nothing comes to my mind. I have limited brain capacity.

We must remember that beauty and worth are subjective. Everyone has unique qualities, and by caring for ourselves and embracing our individuality, we can present our best selves. Instead of comparing, we must focus on self-growth and confidence, boosting our self-esteem and career prospects.

Students and young adults may feel that they are not worthy of being good sons or daughters since they cannot/could not do well as per their parents' expectations. They may feel that God has made them less capable individuals. Several more impressions like these may plague their minds. These barriers make them hesitant to converse confidently with themselves and others.

Almost all of us experience one or more of the above feelings at some point in life but think we are isolated cases. If we understand that what we are going through is simple human psychology, instead of resisting, we should allow it to pass through in a natural way and focus on our goals. Remembering that we don't need to change ourselves to be like someone else is important. Every individual is uniquely talented in their own way. We only need to remove the obstacles within ourselves that are preventing us from making progress.

Many find the self-discovery process painful, fearful, and objectionable. It can even be an agonizing experience, especially when someone has a traumatic past. Open your heart; this is required to remove negative impressions inside you. When you experience this, know that your transformation has begun.

Exercise:

1. Why is it important to find your true self?

___

___

___

2. What are the prime reasons for a person to behave negatively? How can it be eliminated?

___

___

___

3. How do self-induced barriers hinder your growth and happiness? Give a few examples of self-induced barriers.

___

___

___

Chapter 16
Release Negative Attachments

Self-image transformation starts with removing the barriers inside it.

Throughout our lives, we encounter various experiences that leave a lasting impression on us. Some of these impressions are positive, while others are negative. These negative impressions can make it challenging to lead our lives happily. These impressions stem from our emotional responses to the people and places around us. Our emotions act like a thread, connecting our good and bad memories to these individuals and locations.

If we ask someone about a pleasant experience from their past, they will recall it eagerly, cherishing it deeply. Conversely, when reminded of a terrible experience, they often say, "I'd rather forget that." Even though we try to hold onto good experiences and forget the bad ones, we do not make any effort to influence and bring about the required change in our memories.

While positive impressions fuel our progress, negative ones drain us. Releasing bad impressions from our subconscious mind requires a definite process of detachment from the sources of those memories. The objective is to become dispassionate about the negative energies of the past that have been pulling us back. It takes courage to sever all connections with people and places that have validated us negatively. However, it might be necessary for our transformation. Although those we detach from may not understand the changes we are going through, it's important to forgive them and free ourselves from negative emotions. Forgiveness is more for our betterment; it frees up our locked-in power. Doing so heals our mind, body, and spirit, opening new pathways for calm and improved self-esteem despite past trauma or hardships.

As this poetry goes ...

Out of sight, out of mind, out of heart,
It's time to let go, make a brand-new start.
No more pain, no more tears,
No more wasted time, no more fears.
People come and go, that's just life,
But some bring nothing but trouble and strife.
They take, they take, and never give back,
Leaving you drained, feeling under attack.
But you are strong, you are brave,
You deserve love, happiness and peace to pave.
So bid farewell to those who bring pain,
And welcome a new chapter, with love to gain.
Forget their name, forget their face,
Forget their words, forget their place.
Keep them out of sight, out of mind, out of heart,
And focus on you, a brand-new start.

\- Anon

A way to disconnect from your negative life and create a new version of yourself is to become a recluse in your previous world through a complete detachment process and immerse yourself into the new world, focused on personal growth. Many change-makers have used this approach throughout our history. However, because of familial obligations, it may not be practical for everyone to follow this path. Therefore, an equally helpful alternative path to detachment is required.

Follow these steps with full faith to begin your transformation journey.

Steps:

1. Find a quiet place: Relax and centre yourself. Begin the process by making a promise to be truthful and honest with yourself. Identify all the negative emotions within.
2. List the emotions: Write down the name of the person who has hurt you and
3. Recall the incident: remember the event that caused the hurt and identify the negative emotions it generated within you. Journal those negative emotions. Against each name, write the corresponding emotions on a separate sheet of paper.
   Note: You should not force yourself to get the emotion or resist the flow of emotion. Let them flow easily.
   The greater the emotion, the stronger the attachment cord.
4. Embrace abundance: Understand that the world is full of abundance, and you are transforming yourself to align with it. Now, there is no point in

holding on to the negative emotions against people who tried to harm you directly or indirectly. Turn your face towards abundance; everything you desire is available, and you must prepare to receive it.

5. Have a conversation: Close your eyes and have a small conversation with the person. Speak mentally, and although hurt and angry, you are forgiving them and releasing the constrained energy inside you.
   Note: Relieving long-constrained energy can result in crying, tears, and shivers. Let them come freely.
6. Forgive and set them free: Forgive the person completely, saying aloud, "I set you free forever." Repeat this until you genuinely forgive them from your core.
   Note: You will start to feel lighter, and a sense of well-being will set in.
7. Burn the paper: this symbolises cutting out all cords of attachment with that person or place.
8. Pray: Ask God to transform the person into a cheerful soul or a place of positive energy.
9. Repeat the process: Do this for each person and emotion separately.
10. Treat them as strangers: From this point forward. Even if you meet them, treat them as any other unknown individual.

Note: Cultivating positive emotions is important because they contribute to your overall well-being and the development of practical skills that enable you to cope with difficult situations effectively.

Similarly, recall the names of all those you think you have hurt in the past. Using the same process, ask for their forgiveness and seek their blessings. Say, "I forgive myself and absolve myself from all guilt." Repeat until you start feeling lighter inside.

PS: Repeated practice is the key to attaining a state of forgiveness. If the emotional chord is strong, it may take a few more attempts. Be resolute to come out of this process and be relieved. It would be better if these steps were performed at a holy place (a place of your faith) with a pledge and prayer offered to the Almighty. However, if not possible, go to a quiet place where you feel more connected to the divine and perform this process with a relaxed and peaceful mind.

Chapter 17
Understanding Mindfulness

Mindfulness is the essential skill that enables you to lead your life in a focused manner. Without embracing this skill, it would be unjust to encourage you to pursue the other skills discussed for acquiring the SMS rings. In today's fast-paced technological world, mindfulness often gets overlooked.

With the advent of technology and changes in communication style, there is a significant decrease in our attention span. Our mind keeps hovering from one point to another, just grabbing at things that interest us or demand our attention. Even before we finish one, we drift to another thing. There is a constant urge to keep checking messages and replies. The habit has gone so deep into society that the expectancy for a reply or reaction has been reduced to a few minutes. Also, there is a constant urge to remain abreast with news and gain knowledge on the topics one comes across. This kind of Instant gratification reduces our focus.

A study conducted on 200 people, led by Microsoft Canada, on the reduction in people's attention span since the year 2000, reveals that it has reduced from twelve seconds to eight seconds. That's when mobile phones started changing the way we communicate.

Courtesy: Microsoft study claims human attention span now lags behind goldfish 15th May 2015

Engaging too much on a mobile phone has resulted in losing a lot of valuable time, thus making our lives more stressful. The loss of societal values can be seen everywhere. Human relations are suffering, which is further decreasing the quality of life.

A Harvard Gazette states that 47 per cent of the time, we are not paying attention to what we are doing, which means we are not mindful half of the time. This reduces our efficiency in producing results. It is also observed that people are consistently less happy when their minds keep wandering.

Courtesy: Wandering mind, not a happy mind. Harward Gazette

Once we immerse ourselves in the processes dealt with in this book to get a positive and high self-image, we realise that we are naturally required to focus on our thoughts to gain stability and calmness in our approach towards life. Whether it is to get released from negative impressions, develop fundamental attitudes, gain self-awareness, understand our strengths and weaknesses, do the clearing process, and give the proper signal to the mind to build a strong self-image. All of these objectives are based on being mindful of our thoughts and emotions so that we respond to people and situations efficiently. And the bonus is that these activities will keep you engaged and focused, significantly reducing your screen time.

Many people feel that being in the present moment is not their thing. However, the fact that you have read the book to this page with some attention is proof that you can live in the present moment. Each process explained in the book involves living in the present moment. These processes develop a focused approach to life.

Developing the right attitude is necessary for controlling the mind. Building the base of our core with fundamental attitudes is of immense help in developing a focused mind.

A pure mind is a focused mind.

Raaj Sinha

Benefits of Living in the Present Moment

Being in the present is an important aspect of our overall well-being. Mindfulness decreases our anxiety and stress. It improves our immune system and sleep.

It helps increase our focus, creativity, and innovation. It helps us understand the problems of others, thus improving our emotional intelligence. It increases our capability to do things better and more effectively.

Mindfulness is the gateway for developing the rest of our resources. Through mindfulness, we become aware of the present moment and keep assessing whether we are utilizing our time properly. We become mindful of our behaviour and its correctness. If we are not aware of our current state, we may not know which attributes or resources we need to work on.

Mindfulness can help us build an efficient mind by consistently sending positive signals that contribute to developing a uniform core. Positive thoughts align with the core, and negative thoughts are rejected as they do not align with the core. Refer to the chapter on Mind Control and the 'Maker-Checker Diagram' appearing later in the book.

Through mindfulness and meditation techniques, we can train our minds to imbibe positive values such as a sense of ease, warmheartedness, kindness, compassion, and humility toward others. By sensitizing the brain to the positive, we create a uniform and strong core pattern in our subconscious mind. This helps strengthen brain signals and makes our minds faster and more efficient.

Positive emotional experiences broaden our awareness, allowing us to take in more of the world around us. On the other hand, negative emotions like frustration, anxiety, and irritation often lead to a narrowing of our focus. This can be likened to a physical expansion and contraction—when we're in a positive state, we feel open and expansive, while negative emotions can make us feel closed off and restricted.

Imagine walking into a place with a pleasant atmosphere. You feel uplifted and inclined to take in the surroundings, perhaps even pausing to appreciate the details. Conversely, if you were to enter a run-down or unwelcoming space, your instinct might be to leave quickly, wanting to escape the negative environment.

When we reflect on the total time spent being sad until now, we realise that we have lost that part of our lives without doing anything constructive for ourselves. This is because sadness can overshadow positive experiences and make it difficult to recall anything good, which can then sap your energies. The alternative to this would be to remind ourselves that life is beautiful. However, we need to experience life without biases. Recall how happy we were as small children. Finding happiness in the more minor things and seeking reasons to be satisfied, even in challenging circumstances, can help us become more mindful and live in the present moment. This approach can also lead to quicker problem-solving and a more fulfilling life overall, allowing us to experience the equivalent of **multiple lifetimes within a single lifetime.**

Meditative Mode

We don't go into meditation to achieve something; it is a state of surrender and entering the journey the mind takes by using imagination or following well-thought-out instructions.

When we close our eyes and visually disconnect from the world, our attention goes to the thinking mind. We realise how much our mind keeps working continuously. Since no visual signal goes to the mind, it goes into thinking or hearing mode. In thinking mode, the mind thinks of past events or the future. In hearing mode, it becomes sensitive to the surrounding sound.

Do not resist and allow the mind to wander. Respect your mind. Gently but firmly focus on the next set of instructions, or simply follow your breath.

Slowly, the mind calms down and steadies itself to come into the present moment. Our state of mind regulates our breath. If we are anxious or have any negative feelings, it is likely that our breath gets disoriented. Therefore, focusing on the breath steadies it, resulting in a settled mind. It is ready to follow the instructions from outside or the mind itself. Those who do not have experience of meditation may find it difficult to calm their mind. My advice is to select a peaceful place and time to practice it. Mind is most settled when you wake up in the morning or evening, when you are through with your day's work and want to devote some time to the Almighty.

If you have no experience, start with 10 or 15 minutes and gradually increase.

Do the following as you prepare to meditate:

- Do some exercise or yoga, followed by a few minutes of rhythmic breathing.
- [Deep breathing calms down the mind and prepares it for getting focused]
- Be grateful; thank God for everything you have: health, air, water, food, sun, home, family, relationships, and all the essential materials that make your life healthy and safe.
- Sit down and keep your palms open to the sky (ready to receive the energy from the universe).
- Spine erect =>sit straight. Chin at 10 degrees above the normal position, i.e. forehead facing slightly upwards.
- Take a few deep breaths to relax.
- Keep your focus on the breath (inhale and exhale); exhale longer than inhale. You can count numbers from 50 to 1 in reverse order or listen to a sound repeated in some rhythm, like OM, humming, rhythmic drum beats, mantra chants, or any other peaceful sound.
- Let go of everything in your mind. Do not struggle with your wandering mind. Let it wander and feel normal.
- Whatever sounds you hear from the surroundings, let them in. Welcome them.
- Keep a gentle smile on your face. Keep your face upwards with your chin slightly above the normal level. Always feeling the grace of God.
- Refer to the below chart. Follow it for some time. Say 5 to 15 minutes.

- At the end, always open your eyes with gratitude and feeling blessed.

Meditation Flow Chart

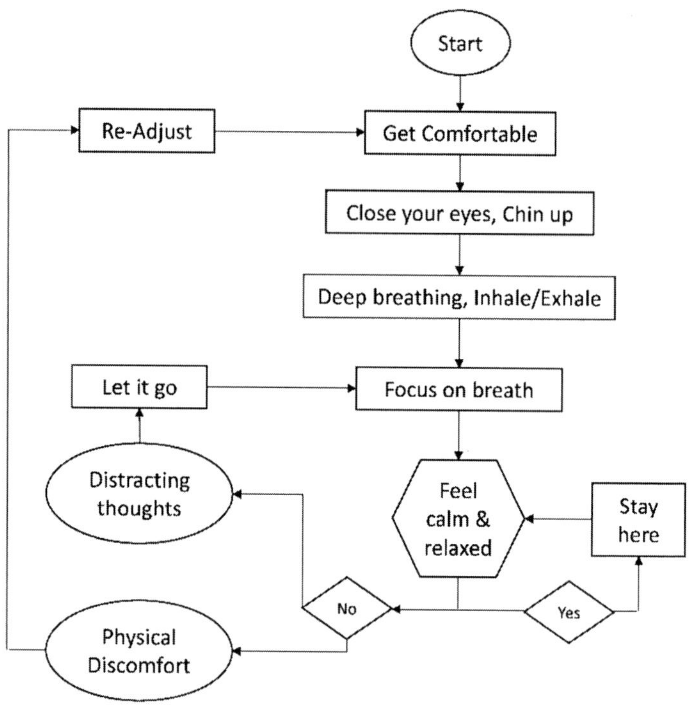

Diagram box representing the process. [Fig 6]

This is the start of meditation, which is settling your mind. Just by doing this, the mind releases all its worry. When we allow our mind to relax, it works more efficiently.

Once you are comfortable doing this step, you can move on to the next steps: visualising goals and tasks and making detailed plans, as enumerated in subsequent chapters.

Chapter 18
Removal of negative patterns

When we say, “Henceforth, I will be calmer,” “I will be positive,” “I will achieve this,” “I will do a better project this time,” “I will write a book,” or “I will be more disciplined,” we should pause to consider whether these are deep thoughts or simply surface-level thoughts. Deep thought is driven by deeply rooted reason.

Many people tend to have generic or surface-level thinking. This kind of thinking doesn't involve deep analysis of the required inputs or actions, making applying it in practical life challenging. In most cases, we struggle to integrate and bring new ideas and approaches into action due to our shallow thinking. On the other hand, deep-level thinking will result in getting the ultimate reason and the desire for change. This can happen when we build a strong self-image. It makes the person in being honest to understand their present state and walk on the right path to achieve the goals for their set mission.

Therefore, we need to change our core by removing negative patterns. These patterns have made the nuclei complicated and hinder clear and robust functioning. These negative patterns are also responsible for negative behaviours.

This reconstruction of a new core by releasing negative patterns from the core will be done by presenting intense desire and emotions to change ourselves.

What are we holding on to?

We must realize that our negative patterns are not truly our own. They are either imposed on us by others or perceived by us as our own, and we mistakenly accept them as our defining characteristics. Therefore, it is entirely pointless to cling to something that does not belong to us. Yet, we often do so unconsciously.

People tend to construct a complex image of themselves based on the judgments and behaviours of others, and this image can hinder their growth. If we had understood earlier in life that accepting negative emotions and judgments creates a negative self-image, we likely would not have internalized them.

For example, a person constantly hearing that they are not good at communicating may materialize this belief, leading to a lack of confidence and opportunities. Similarly, someone repeatedly told they're not creative may avoid certain pursuits, believing that they are not capable and deserving. These shape our limitations and potential.

Ask yourself, "Why am I clinging to those negative ideas about myself?"

You don't need to carry them within yourself. A wrong perception of oneself is the cause of pain and agony in one's life.

By accepting these negative beliefs, you actually give up on the path of improving yourself. You thought it was beyond you; accordingly, an image is formed in your core with those limitations.

It's important to recognize the impact of external judgments on our self-perception. A helpful affirmation to consider is: "I have accepted negative judgments or suggestions from others due to my lack of awareness about their effects. No one has the authority to determine my worth, and I now choose to return all negative judgments to their source with love."

A common question regarding positive validations is: Should we also disregard those? The answer is 'No'. Positive judgments and emotions play a crucial role in our development. They reinforce our core beliefs and contribute to leading fulfilling and successful lives, both in the present and the future.

That's why the saying goes, *Write your bad times in sand and good times in stone.*

Henceforth, don't take negative judgments to heart. The phrase "don't mind" means don't internalize it.

It's important to remember that people who judge you don't necessarily have the ability to evaluate your entire life. They don't know what changes you can make in future. Their judgment is based on their own knowledge and parameters, which are primarily formed by the circumstances. Circumstances may change. What may seem factual at one point in time may not be permanently true about you.

For example, if you don't qualify for the final round of a tournament, it doesn't mean you're not good enough. It simply means that, at that moment, you didn't perform as well as those who did qualify based on the tournament's parameters and rules. Remember, this is just one moment in time, and there will be many more opportunities to succeed.

Likewise, if a student aspiring to pass an exam fails to do so, it simply means that they have not provided the correct answers. It can be assumed that their knowledge of the subject or required skills may have been insufficient compared to those who passed. However, it does not imply that these candidates are forever deemed inadequate and rated low for their entire life!

Take these contrasting examples: John F Kennedy became president of the USA at 43, while Joe Biden became president at 77 years old. Malala Yousafzai became a Nobel Peace laureate at 17 years old, while Mother Teresa was 69 when she was honoured with the same award. William Lawrence Bragg got the Nobel Prize in Physics at age 25, while Arthur Ashkin received it at 96. Everybody has their time zone. Some may find their path and start achieving targets early in life, while others may take much longer. Only those who stop striving fail to attain their goal.

Let Go Process

Subconsciously, we recognize that our ability to think and take action enables us to survive and accomplish many tasks because of the image we carry for ourselves inside. Therefore, we hold tightly to our self-image. Through self-awareness, we understand that by holding onto our self-image, we also hold on to the associated negative attachments and patterns. We are often unaware whether these attachments are the source of worry and stress. Once we identify these negative attachments, we work to release them from our image core.

The process of transformation involves a complete overhaul of our self-image. We must let go of our old, limiting beliefs and embrace a new, empowering perspective about life. We must first realize our negative patterns to begin changing our complex self-image.

Identify your negative thinking patterns, such as labelling people or yourself as stupid, over-generalising, magnifying issues, jumping to conclusions, over-emotion, disregarding positives, excessive fear, snitching, biased approach, etc. These may lead to negative behaviour traits such as gossiping, complaining, being untrustworthy, lacking self-discipline, being unmotivated and low energy, bullying, verbal abuse, rudeness, procrastination, etc. Write them down and reflect on how they hinder your development. Also, mention how you are improving upon it. Pin this list as a reminder of what needs to be improved. Put that paper on the wall, where you can see it frequently and realise what is to be enhanced within your character.

We can gain awareness about our negative patterns through **mindfulness** techniques or by being in silence and analysing ourselves at the end of each day. We analyse how these negative patterns are affecting our growth journey. Every day before you go to sleep, recall your behaviour in several interactions that happened during the day. List them out in your diary. Segregate the positive and negative ones to create awareness in ourselves. See on a daily basis how you are improving on them. Note down in your attitude journal your wins or losses and the lessons you have learned.

An Exercise to release negative patterns:

Another effective way to release patterns from our core is to go into a calm and centred state of mind. We can signal the release of all negative patterns through focused attention. Ultimately, they dissociate from the core and dissolve into eternity, allowing us to move forward unencumbered by the weight of past negative experiences and limiting beliefs.

- Have the list of your negative thinking patterns and behaviour, go through them and remember.

- Find a relaxing place to start the process. You can lie down or sit comfortably on a floor mat or chair.
- Focus on your breath as you inhale and exhale. Close your eyes.
- Our breath is a gift from God that keeps us alive; respect and love it. Imagine that each inhale energizes your body while every exhale relaxes it. Take a moment to show gratitude to the Almighty for this precious gift, and continue for a minute or two.
- Then, progressively tense and relax each part of your body. Start by tensing your feet for three seconds, and then relax.

Do this in sequence, progressively moving up the body, viz. legs, stomach, back, shoulder, face and head.

Note: As you tense and relax the part of your body, talk to them and bless them for doing excellent work.

- Feel every part of your body relaxed and at ease. Stay the same for a few moments.

  Envision your self-image as a complex core surrounded by concentric circles. Visualize chains holding the barriers and patterns together. Identify the various barriers and negative patterns that you have already listed. Visualize them without exerting extra effort. Embrace the process and remain focused on your breath.

  Note: Although we have completed the step of removing negative attachments and barriers, if you don't see your barriers while performing this step, visualize your negative patterns and go ahead.

- Now, imagine breathing into your image core.
- As the air enters your core, picture it expanding like a stretchable balloon. With each breath, feel the core and the concentric circles surrounding it also expand. Continue this for one minute, noticing how the patterns and barriers become tight and tense as your core expands.
- As you focus on the rhythm of your incoming breath, feel the core expanding continuously. Imagine your barriers and negative patterns disengaging from the shackles, disintegrating, and scattering away into the vast space like dust.
- Feel the sense of ease and lightness as you see them getting dissolved into space. Take a few deep breaths, and you'll start to feel lighter. Thank God for the process.
- Now, visualize the circles of the self-image expanding faster.
- Every fifteen seconds, they encompass the room, then the building, then the city, the country, the earth, and finally, the universe.
- Feel that you are part of the universe.
- Picture aligning yourself with the universe's energies, giving you immense relief and relaxation.
- Lie motionless and feel the moment of freedom that will be etched in your memory.
- Now, focus on your core. Your core is now free of barriers and negative patterns. It is fresh, beaming with the universe's energy, ready to embrace positivity and growth.

Note: If your mind wanders during the process, do not worry. Gently bring your focus back to your breath. By showing no resistance to the wandering mind, you show respect to your mind. You will gradually gain focus as you keep practising regularly for 21 days. Do not give up.

Gently bringing back the wandering mind to the process without any internal force is a great step towards developing a good personality.

The diagram of the core with negative patterns and the core with negative patterns released. [Fig 7]

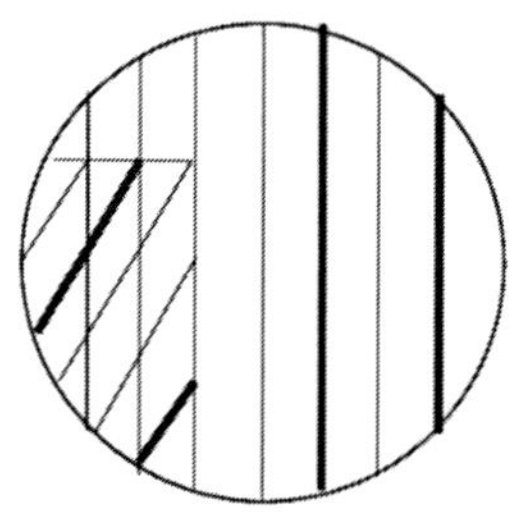

Image Core with Negative Pattern

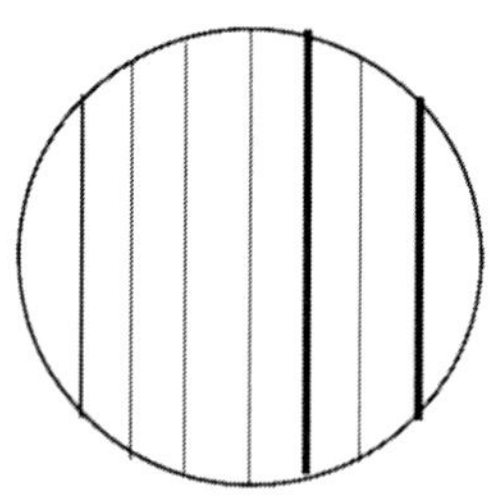

Image Core with Negative Pattern Released

[Fig 7]

Recalling Einstein's words would be apt: "A human being is part of the whole called by us universe, a part limited in time and space. He experiences himself, his thoughts and feelings as something separate from the rest, an optical illusion of consciousness. This delusion is a prison for us, restricting us to our personal desires and affection for a few persons nearest to us. Our task must be to free ourselves from this prison by widening our circle of compassion to embrace all living creatures and the whole of nature and its beauty. The feeling of being part of a larger community gives us our purpose and strength to contribute."

Exercise:

1. What is surface level thinking?

____

____

____

2. How does the process of letting go help us remove negative patterns and barriers?

____

____

____

3. How does the let-go process enhance our energy level and make us more relevant to the world?

____

____

____

4. List down the behaviour patterns that have been hindering your growth.

____

____

____

Chapter 19
Fundamental Skills: Developing the Core Base

Establishing a solid foundation is essential for transforming into a new self-image. The term "foundation" speaks for itself: building a strong base that will withstand the challenges life throws at us from time to time. Have you ever wondered what we remember about a person: wealth or character? Whether a leader in politics or business, it is often the character that we talk about.

Having certain skills can temporarily boost self-esteem as you gain expertise and recognition. Society may also perceive you as a successful individual. However, true happiness and fulfilment can remain elusive without a solid foundation, resulting in disappointment and recurring pain.

History offers examples of leaders with excellent skills who lacked fundamental attitudes, resulting in their downfall. In the great Hindu mythology epic 'Ramayana', Ravana, the king of Lanka, possessed immense power and invincibility. Yet, his lack of love, compassion and open acceptance led to his downfall. Such personalities are termed evil. Their arrogant behaviour inflicts more pain on themselves and others.

The same principles apply in the business world. A business thrives when its societal and moral values promote the well-being of investors, employees, and customers alike. A company that cheats investors or customers does not last long. A weak foundation eventually reveals selfish intentions, leading to failure. A business that falsely inflates its balance sheet to deceive investors or reduces product quality to increase profits may not be acceptable to customers and, sooner or later, face their disapproval. Examples of balance sheet falsification include Enron, WorldCom, AIG, and Lehman Brothers.

Persons with a weak core often find themselves at a disadvantage over time, as this lack of internal strength can lead to significant challenges. Individuals lacking resilience may struggle to cope effectively when pressures arise—be it in personal relationships, professional environments, or life's unexpected hurdles. Their inability to withstand stress can unveil their underlying selfish intentions, which typically become apparent sooner or later.

In moments of adversity, someone with a fragile character may falter quickly, demonstrating their inability to maintain composure or make sound decisions. This reaction highlights their struggles and serves as a tangible reminder of their weak personality. Ultimately, the true nature of such individuals is revealed under pressure, reminding the importance of developing a robust inner foundation that can withstand life's inevitable trials.

A Healthy Base:

Repeating it, A healthy mind resembles a child in many ways. It is incredibly observant, listening carefully to the world around it. Like a child, a healthy mind is resilient in pursuing its goals, eagerly striving for success, and unwaveringly confident in its abilities. It is open-minded, free from prejudice, and unburdened by unnecessary concerns.

We were all children once. It is a reminder that each of us has these attributes in the base.

Let us recall the key attributes of a happy and successful person and keep them in mind as we go forward.

<u>The key elements of a successful personality include:</u>

Self-awareness: Ability to look inside and recognize the area for improvement positively.

Good Health: Efficient working of the mind and body.

Courageous: One who does not fear facing new challenges.

Resilience: Staying focused on the goal even in adversity.

Sound Communication: Conveying messages effectively with clarity and purpose.

Believe: Having faith in oneself to achieve set goals.

Acceptance: Gratitude to the almighty for past and present, aligning with the laws of the universe. Also, not becoming critical about anything.

Patience: Wisdom to understand that some things take time to unfold.

Compassion: Concern for others' pain or worries.

Practising open acceptance, non-judgment, patience, and compassion

Adopting these attitudes offers two significant benefits. First, they enable us to exercise self-control and direct our attention toward what truly matters. Second, they enhance our ability to remain present and engaged with our surroundings, fostering a greater awareness of our current circumstances and actions.

Cultivating these fundamental attitudes requires a conscious and deliberate direction of our attention. Daily, if we analyse, we see ourselves presenting behaviours that may not be as per the ideal image we have in mind for the envisioned personality. It would be better if we keep aligning ourselves with the right personality. However, thoughts of aligning ourselves to the proper behaviour may not come to our mind, or we keep giving such thoughts a pass, thinking they are unrelated to our targets and goals. What we don't realise is that subconsciously, this lax attitude may affect our self-image negatively.

Therefore, a better way to keep correcting ourselves is to become a detached observer of our perceptions, thoughts, and emotions. By witnessing our behaviour in this way, we can spend more time analysing our experiences and learn to take less personally what happens in our bodies and minds. This approach helps to increase our understanding of thoughts, emotions, behaviour and context that push us into reactivity.

We learn how we lose focus on our day-to-day objectives and how the goal of life drifts away from us, making us more anxious and unhappy. This understanding is an essential step in breaking free from habitual behaviours and mental ruts that have been plaguing us in the past.

Open Acceptance

In the previous chapter, we did an exercise that helped us improve our sense of open acceptance through meditation techniques. We connected with the universe by expanding our minds and becoming a part of it, thereby bringing ourselves into unison, i.e., total acceptance of things as they are.

Whenever we come across something or someone that doesn't meet our expectations, we usually spend a lot of our energy imagining how to change it. Unfortunately, this kind of thinking often leads to negativity and drains our energy. A better approach is to accept things as they are without judgment or resistance. By being receptive to all emotions, whether joy, sorrow, hope, or despair, we can live in harmony. This approach lets us focus our energy on our goals and promotes harmony and society's development. In short, open acceptance allows us to establish deep interpersonal relationships and live a more fulfilling life. The attitude of open acceptance improves relationships among people. We understand that getting offended or irked by someone’s behaviour does not justify lowering our own etiquette or behavioural standards. Maintaining a respectful demeanour, even in challenging situations, reflects our values and promotes a harmonious environment. Dealing such issues with acceptance can have a positive effect on that person as well.

Every day, we waste a lot of time discussing issues that we are hardly inclined to do anything about. These issues may relate to politics, administration, sports, or any other topic from the news media. People show rigid opinions on matters they might not be fully updated on, but tend to fall into discussions and fret over. We must be aware of the time we spend shooting the breeze and not focusing on our goals. Suppose that we realise that getting into a discussion would be fruitless and that we would lose time in achieving our daily targets. In that case, our open acceptance attitude will allow us to move on from such situations. It has helped me save time in the office and my personal life.

Open acceptance also helps when dealing with a child who is not focused on their studies. Parents tend to become irritable and show anger, which may lead to two outcomes: one, the child becomes fearful of the situation and begins to give up; and second, they might learn to handle challenges in an unhealthy way. Instead, if we show understanding toward the child and treat them with the same respect that we would offer to our friends, the child would be more likely to open up about their problems.

Similarly, in any relationship, especially between spouses, practising open acceptance fosters peace and cooperation, helping to build a happy and healthy relationship.

Non-Judging

We tend to judge every aspect of our experience. We generally form pictures or opinions on things through our understanding. We feel happy when we find anything in conformance to it, and non-conformance would result in discontent or unhappy feelings. However, wisdom comes from realizing that we may lack complete knowledge of it and, therefore, choosing our actions accordingly. But then, knowledge is never complete, and therefore, in most cases, judging can land us in uncomfortable situations. A fact that most of us remain unaware of.

We should observe our judging tendencies like an external monitor to avoid this. When we do that, we see how detrimental it can be to be caught up in our ideas, opinions, likes, and dislikes.

Suspending judgment allows us to remain curious and open-minded, leading to making more informed decisions. A strong foundation at our core helps us avoid a closed-minded approach and enhances our decision-making skills. This attitude is subtle and should be understood from the proper perspective. In professional life, we are required to make quick decisions under a particular situation based on our judgement, and therefore, it may seem contrary to the above approach, but actually, it's not. Instead, this attitude helps us make well-informed decisions that don't hurt us later.

However, if our foundation is weak, we cannot make the right decisions at the right time.

A small incident during a train journey...

On a train, two children were running around, getting into fights and disturbing passengers.

Lost in thoughts, the father occasionally smiled at them but didn't intervene. One traveller, irritated, confronted their father about this lack of discipline, "What kind of a father are you? The children are misbehaving, and instead of stopping them, you are encouraging them with your smiles. Isn't it your responsibility to make them understand how to behave?"

The father paused briefly and said, "I am just thinking about how to explain it to them, brother."

The traveller said, "What do you mean? I don't understand?"

The man said, "My wife had gone to her maternal home. She passed away yesterday due to an accident. I am taking the children there for the final rites, and now I don't know how to confess the truth. I'm confused about how to explain to them that they will never see their mother again." Hearing this, everyone was stunned. The children continued with their playful antics, running around in the compartment. The passengers who were initially frustrated suddenly fell silent and were filled with compassion. The father's demeanour, once seen as negligent, now revealed a profound sorrow as he shouldered the responsibilities of a single parent and was saddened by the separation of his life partner.

Our perception of others can change instantly, leading to a sudden change in our attitude. This reminds us not to judge others hastily and to approach situations with understanding.

It's important to recognize the judging mind in our daily life. So, if you are in a workshop or doing meditation, you find yourself thinking – "This is boring," or "I can't do this," realize that this is your mind judging the experience. Try to notice the feeling that is occurring and how it has been evoked in you.

When we can observe our experience without wanting it to be different from what it is, we take a tremendous step in alleviating the hardship of life. This is also a way to develop ease in our lives.

Patience

Another basic attitude to build as a foundation in our core is patience. In today's frantically paced world, everybody seems to be in a hurry to solve an issue or complete a task. The day is filled with a To-do list without proper time assessment. When things go wrong, we often expect quick fixes for our problems, but not everything can be rushed. In growing the skill of patience, we better understand and accept that some things must unfold in their own time. Some of you will likely become impatient in attaining a new self-image. But if we invite patience into our practice, we can bring self-compassion, helping us acknowledge and accept our developmental process, trusting that our evolution is unfolding exactly as it should. It takes nine months for a child to be born and study for sixteen years to get a graduation degree, but we rush immediately to earn money. The mad rush to get quick money adds a lot of stress to people's lives. Everything has a gestation period before it bears fruit. There are two types of patience: one that is required during the long period of endeavour before we get the desired result, and the other is behavioural calm that we exhibit when we are waiting for our turn in a queue at a ticket counter or getting delayed due to a late running flight, train, etc. The patience shown during such circumstances is a test of our character.

I don't mean to say that patience is a passive word and that we don't need to do anything but wait. I only want to emphasize that to achieve your goals, keep working hard every day and be patient with yourself to get the result of your hard work. Do not jump from one unfinished work to another and then another and another. Your focus on your work improves if you have patience with yourself.

An important aspect of being wise is to know the prudent application of this skill of patience.

Raaj Sinha

Parents must be patient in nurturing and guiding their children, as good changes take some time to manifest.

Patience works wonders for removing stress from life. When you realise that nothing is permanent, you become more tolerant, forgiving, and less judgmental.

BE AWARE, KEEP WORKING AND WAIT FOR THE RIGHT MOMENT

This is always easier said than done; inculcating patience requires some practice, as suggested in mind control exercises later in this book. Becoming a distanced impartial observer of our behaviour to understand mind reactivity is an excellent tool to have throughout the day to help us become more patient. With this awareness, we can learn to respond more skilfully to challenging situations and cultivate inner peace and balance even in difficult situations.

Remember, whether you complete a project in record time, learn something new, or discover something, patience plays a crucial role in producing excellent outcomes.

If you keep your thinking process simple, remain truthful, disciplined, and always ready to give 100 per cent, you can deliver great service to society, no matter where you are in your life journey.

Always have a positive attitude. ...An Inspiring Story

The Difference between job and work

Cape Town's uneducated surgeon, Mr Hamilton, who was awarded the honorary degree in of Master of Medicine, could neither read nor write.

Cape Town Medical University is a leading medical institution. The world's first bypass operation took place at the same university.

One morning in 2003, world-renowned surgeon Professor David Dent announced in the university auditorium, "Today we are awarding an honorary degree in medicine to the man who produced the most surgeons in the world. Who is this extraordinary teacher and an amazing surgeon who studied medical science and surprised the human mind?"

With this, the professor announced the name "Hamilton", and the entire auditorium applauded! It was the most significant reception in the history of this university.

Hamilton was born in Sanitani, a remote village in Cape Town. His parents were shepherds. He wore goat skin and walked on the mountains barefoot all day. When his father fell ill, he moved to Cape Town to support his ailing father.

Construction was underway at the University of Cape Town, and he worked as a labourer there for many years. When the construction process ended, he got the job of mowing the tennis court, which he did for three years.

Then arrived a strange turn in his life, and he reached a point in medical science that no one else had ever been.

It was a mild, warm morning. Professor Robert Joyce, who was researching giraffes, wanted to find out why a giraffe doesn't have a seizure when it bends down his neck to drink water.

They laid a giraffe on the operating table with anaesthesia, but as soon as the operation started, the giraffe shook its head.

The professor came out of the theatre. He saw Hamilton was mowing the lawn in front. The professor noticed that he was a healthy young man of strong stature. They beckoned him and ordered him to grab the giraffe's neck.

The operation lasted eight hours. During this time, the doctor took short breaks. However, Hamilton continued holding its neck. When the operation was over, he quietly went out and started mowing the lawn. The next day, the professor called him again. He came and stood holding the giraffe's neck in place, after which it became his routine.

He worked double for many months. He neither demanded additional compensation nor complained.

Professor Robert Joyce, impressed by his perseverance and sincerity, promoted him from a mower of the tennis court to a lab assistant. He now came to the university, went to the operating theatre and helped the surgeons. This process continued for several years.

In 1958 came another turning point in his life. This year, Dr Bernard came to the university and started heart transplant operations. Hamilton became his assistant, and during these operations, he went from being an assistant to an additional surgeon.

Now, the doctors would operate, and after the operation, Hamilton was given the task of stitching. He used to do excellent stitches. He stitched on fifty people in one day. While working in the operating theatre, he began to understand the human body more than surgeons. So, the senior doctors gave him the responsibility of teaching the junior doctors.

He now began teaching surgery techniques to junior doctors. He gradually became the most important figure in the university.

In 1970, the third turning point in his life occurred when research on the liver began. He identified one such liver artery during the process, which made liver transplantation easier.

His remarks astonished the great minds of medical science.

"Hamilton" achieved this position with sincerity and perseverance. He was associated with the University of Cape Town for 50 years, during which he never took a vacation.

He would leave his home at three o'clock at night, walk fourteen miles to the university, and enter the theatre at exactly six o'clock. People used to fix their watches with his impeccable timing.

He received an honour that no one in medical science has ever earned. He was the first illiterate teacher in medical history and the first illiterate surgeon to train 30,000 surgeons in his lifetime.

He passed away in 2005 and was buried at the university. After receiving their degree, graduate surgeons were required to visit his grave before entering practical life.

Do you know how he got this position?

With only one word, 'Yes'.

The day he was called to the operation theatre to grab the giraffe's neck. He could have refused that day and said, "I am a Grounds Maintenance Worker and my job is not to hold the giraffe's neck." Had he a judging mind, making this fabulous history wouldn't have been possible.

He showed immense patience. Even after his work as a mower, he stayed back and focused on the additional work of holding the giraffe for long hours at a stretch. He continued for several years just doing the same thing.

Every job in the world has specific criteria, and those jobs are available only to those who meet the criteria. While if you wanted to do work, you could start any work in the world in a few minutes and no power in the world would be able to stop you.

"Hamilton" had found the secret; he valued the work rather than the job. Thus, his discovery changed the history of medical science.

Imagine if he had applied for a surgeon's job. Would he have become a surgeon? Never. But he put the lawn mower down, held the giraffe's neck, and became a surgeon.

People generally look for a job, not for work. The day we start behaving like Hamilton, we will win great laurels and become successful.

What is your attitude when you are asked to take on some extra responsibilities? Or how do you feel when you are unable to meet the timelines?

If you think the work is difficult or not meant for you and still keep doing it, you will soon feel tired. Find your work and enjoy it.

No career or future planning is helpful if basic attitudes are not sorted first.

Exercise:

1. How does open acceptance help us remain focused on our goals?

   ____

   ____

   ____

2. What are the two types of patience? Give some examples where our patience is tested in day-to-day life.

   ____

   ____

   ____

3. List your present behaviour patterns that do not align with the core values.

   ____

   ____

   ____

4. For each one, apply the external monitor technique of becoming an observer of your behaviour daily. Every week, assess the outcome changes in your behaviour. Maintain the chart as a part of your daily routine.

____

____

____

5. Do you love what you are pursuing in your life presently?

____

____

____

Chapter 20
Application of fundamental skills at work

Dear past, thanks for all the lessons. Dear Future, I am ready.

I am mentally and emotionally ready to enter a new phase in my life. I am prepared to grow and get better every day.

This chapter will discuss some vital skills that help us excel in our careers and personal lives. While reviewing these skills, you will realise that the fundamental skills developed at the core of our self-image help immensely in acquiring these additional behavioural skills.

There are two reasons for explaining some of the practical life skills. One is to give you an idea of why building the base of our image core with fundamental attitudes is essential, and the second is to realise the importance of honing these practical skills for your overall success. These skills are relevant to both professional and personal contexts.

When taught in the business world, these practical skills aim to develop the ability to navigate positively through social and business networks, find new creative ideas, build relationships and networks, persuade others, persevere through all the ups and downs, and create value for others. Thus, it helps you achieve your organisational goals.

Leadership skills are often associated with upper management and are sometimes seen as traits reserved for those in leadership roles or as a specific profession. However, this can lead to confusion about who can develop and benefit from these skills.

As a proponent of adequately educating children, I think all moral stories taught in the school's primary section were supposed to build the foundation for these skills. Still, these lessons often fade as we grow older. These stories somehow fail to impact an individual's thinking process. We fail to understand that those lessons are the foundation for a successful individual and society. If you fail to reflect these values in your day-to-day behaviour, you may hinder yourself from becoming a successful and happy individual. These skills start paying dividends from the start of your career.

Leadership skills can be demonstrated at every stage of life. These skills shouldn't just be a part of our education but also a way of life within society. Additionally, maintaining discipline in our practices is crucial for achieving our goals.

Exuberating positivity and energy are essential to these skills.

Creating Influence

In our day-to-day lives, we face situations when we need to convince others, whether at work or in life in general.

We can influence and motivate others to work towards a common goal through our clarity of thought. This skill is very important in running a business efficiently or getting the team to work towards a goal.

The first step in making an influence in society or a group is communication— both verbal and non-verbal. Positive vibes of a person create an interaction that positively influences the other person. A person with a high self-image can uplift others with every gesture, inflection and interaction. Caring and a 'giver attitude' should be reflected every time you interact. Open-acceptance, the core behaviour of our self-image, makes us acquire the attitude of humility and compassion.

Humility and transparency create the highest level of influence, which in turn builds trust, which is the foundation of any relationship. **Remember that people will forgive many things where trust exists but rarely forgive anything where trust is absent**.

Based on my industry observations, I strongly believe that humility, empathy, and truthfulness are essential traits that should be central to our character. If you aim to create influence within your organization, horizontally or vertically, there is nothing better than demonstrating humility and compassion with everyone you interact with. Empathetic communicators exhibit authenticity and transparency, which are absent in those who communicate behind a carefully crafted façade of a fragile ego.

Allow me to narrate this small instance:

During one of our annual performance reviews, the company's executive director joined us for the first time. There were around twenty-five people in the room, and as he shook hands with each of us, he addressed everyone by name. It was as if he knew each of us, which was a pleasant surprise. His approach immediately grabbed our attention. In his short speech, he mentioned the engagement and time devoted by all to ensuring the project progresses ahead of schedule and how this kind of engagement might affect the daily lives of all of us. He said, "We cannot compensate for the time you have missed with your families, but we will ensure they aren't overburdened. Apart from paying a project allowance, we would like you to bring your family to our milestone celebrations. We want to reward your families as well." We all felt enthused.

Though it is not practical for everyone to remember the names of each of our team members, we can make everyone feel special with whom we interact.

"Names are the sweetest and most important sound in any language".

Addressing people as groups using words like "You all" or "All of them" does not help build close relationships. When giving compliments, it's always better to address individuals rather than groups, as they feel privileged and acknowledged better. Later, they may even become your close acquaintances.

On the other hand, if you have to give negative feedback, you do not point out a particular person but instead make a subtle remark in general. Remember not to say anything that makes you lose the support of the entire group. That's a loss in your effort to build connections. People who are clear in their viewpoints while remaining compassionate to people gain respect in their communities.

"Your humility and compassion are exhibited more when you address one-on-one".

Raaj Sinha

Main Principles for Gaining Influence:

- Don't criticize, condemn or complain [Apply non-judgement]
- If you are wrong, admit it. [Truthfulness]
- Talk about others' interests. [Show compassion]
- Give others their space [Apply open-acceptance]

- Let others save face [show humility and empathy]

Avoid belittling others

Berating someone is not looked upon as a healthy thought. Its long-term effect is far more harmful. In an ever-changing world, you would never know that the path to your success or endeavour has to cross through the person you once criticised. Whom you sullied once can become your collaborator. To remain flexible, you should refrain from forming opinions that hinder your progress in future. The fundamental attitude of "non-judging" is essential.

We follow a respectful and courteous approach in the corporate world while dealing with external stakeholders. However, this approach is sometimes taken lightly when it comes to our team. Seniors tend to belittle their juniors at the slightest instance to demonstrate their superiority. Unfortunately, this type of working culture has penetrated our society deeply and is one of the main reasons for low productivity across industries. Though company rules nowadays strictly prohibit such behaviour, there is still some distance to go before we see a consistent culture across companies where senior employees show genuine respect and support towards their juniors.

Calm your mind first:

It's important to calm your mind before communicating with others. If you're distressed or upset, take a moment to collect yourself before proceeding. Remember, applying 'Momentus'. It is explained in the chapter "Mind Control, later in this book. When you do respond, remember not to speak negatively about anyone, as it doesn't help or attract people. Maintaining your composure is important when you feel angry or annoyed. Don't let your emotions get the best of you, especially in public, as you may regret it later. Effective influencers have adeptly honed the ability to restrain their expressions and set aside their pride, particularly during instances of negative emotions. Always strive to make others feel that you are positive, progressive, and in control by choosing your words carefully and focusing on making things better moving forward. Apply open acceptance and drop negative emotions, saying to yourself, '*Never Mind.*'

Open up dialogues with those who challenge and develop you; **value the discussion, not the opinion**. But if you are being denigrated, move out of the discussion and place, if possible.

Being a keen Listener:

In this age of instant communication, everyone seems to be in such a rush to communicate what's on their mind without patiently listening to others. We may not realise that we may miss out on valuable insights from others. Silence, with attentive observation, is a powerful tool. This gives us immense capability to make informed decisions. You will better understand why and how decisions should be made and can develop a clear strategy for getting things done.

The power of listening is the most desirable thing people want from us. Doing so may open the gateway to changing hearts and minds. Listening well creates an instant impression and lays the foundation for a trustworthy relationship in the future.

In the present age, most people will say, "I do not have time to listen." People crave to be heard and understood, but few take the time to listen. When you offer to listen, it creates an instant connection.

In the corporate world, many companies still lack this culture. The phrase “Boss is always right” remains highly common. Employees are expected to follow orders without question. Some managers try to listen to their teams, but the company’s culture limits this. Suggestions to improve processes or business might be welcomed, but they are often suppressed by policies that favour the company's traditional culture. Companies are still very protective of issues related to employee welfare. They prefer copying other organizations rather than becoming pioneers in their welfare policies.

Organizations thrive when there is harmony, where employee participation is actively encouraged in policy matters related to employee policies and business growth. Loyal employees, in turn, engage in meaningful conversations with customers to understand their needs and develop products and services to serve them better. However, the responsibility lies with the company to foster a culture of obtaining necessary feedback.

As discussed earlier, progress depends on genuine support from others. It is crucial to win people’s hearts by understanding them, whether in your business or within your team in an organization.

Remember, to understand people’s needs, you must listen to them and build a trustworthy relationship. Only after gaining understanding can you discuss matters relevant to them. In business, this enables you to offer suitable products and services. Consistent listening and understanding are essential for engaging with others about what they care about.

Trying to gain influence in others' lives through showmanship or manipulation doesn’t work. Therefore, we need to express **humility and empathy** in a genuine manner.

Any expression driven by self-propagation may not be well received by others. When you come to know a person's ulterior motives, the relationship is forever doomed.

Don't lose the opportunity to acknowledge and appreciate:

We should never miss the chance to affirm people for their good deeds. Our words significantly influence the lives of those around us. Spoken affirmations can inspire hope, encouragement, and self-esteem in our families, friends, and others.

However, opportunities to genuinely affirm or bless others pass us by every day. No doubt, we all notice someone who looks especially nice or has done a great job on something, but too often, we let it go unnoticed. Most of us know firsthand how deflating it can be to accomplish something or go out of our way for someone – only to have it overlooked. Yet, if someone says, "You did a great job!" we feel warm, appreciated, and validated. Positive affirmations empower us to take risks, take chances, and do our best.

It's not always natural to speak out loud about the good thoughts we have about others. Instead, we might find it easier to hold onto our judgements and criticisms. Adjusting our attitudes and focusing on the positive qualities of others helps the individual stay positive.

So, make it a point to speak words that bless, encourage, inspire and uplift. Let's focus on the positive qualities of our friends, peers, and everyone else. Praise them for their strengths, affirming the character traits that we appreciate.

Even a fool can criticise, condemn and complain. But it takes character and self-control to be understanding and forgiving. Let's find reasons behind their actions and help them overcome them. This instils sympathy and kindness and makes the relationship a better understood one.

Building Relationships

Many individuals fail to prioritise the importance of building and maintaining strong relationships during their teenage or young adult years. In some cases, they may even ignore the role of their parents in their lives. It's common for the younger generation to believe that the older generation has little to offer. While it's true that they have limited knowledge of today's world, they still possess the timeless core values that are essential to leading a meaningful life. It's crucial to instil these values—such as the importance of building and maintaining relationships in children from a young age and emphasizing the significance of holding onto them throughout their lifetime.

Chapter 21
Building the Image Core: Finding Your Purpose

Whether you enjoy doing a few things instinctively or develop skills to do them and find pleasure in doing so as you progress, it should ultimately align with your values and principles. Otherwise, you may start to feel tired sooner or later. You will eventually realise that the only reason for doing the job was to support your family or yourself, meaning remaining in survival mode and living in fear.

In the 'Developing the Base' section, we learned the core values to embed in our image core. For true success, we must apply these core values to who we aspire to be (our purpose).

Finding your purpose is like discovering the true fragrance within you to which your mind feels most energised to work throughout the day. This involves identifying your strengths and weaknesses and finding the work that makes your life more meaningful. A work that fascinates you so much that you are ready to **learn lifelong**. Doing the work gives you personal wellness, and there is harmony inside and around you, aiding you to do more of what you are doing.

"Discovery of the self can mean the difference between success and failure."

T F James

Many of us never engage in this process and instead let life unfold naturally, doing our best within the circumstances we encounter.

Only a few fortunate individuals discover it early in life through their own calling. Their parents or close ones recognise the child's dedication and support them in pursuing their path with focus. Such minds exhibit clear core patterns and produce strong signals for action.

For most people, this internal call is weak, possibly due to fear, doubt, or negative validation at some point. It is suppressed and does not emerge confidently. Without a strong internal voice, the mind is influenced by external ideas and suggestions that can complicate the core pattern. We begin our journey by following the path set by or borrowed from others. In such cases, it may be a coincidence if our purpose aligns with the inner fragrance.

No matter where we are in life, it is always beneficial to explore ourselves and plan a future accordingly.

Self-discovery can only occur when we have developed sufficient self-awareness, i.e., knowledge about ourselves. After removing your barriers and negative patterns, you can uncover your genuine strengths. What brings you inner peace or joy? Which work allows you to connect with your true self? What inherent skills do you possess? By the way, inherent skills are those that come naturally—at least some part of them.

The self-discovery process requires a calm and reflective mind detached from daily routine, jobs and worries. It is always good to do this type of exercise after taking a break from our regular routine. A peaceful and settled mind helps in our thinking process. Pay attention to things you naturally love doing. List them out on paper. By paying attention to the subconscious pull for these activities, you can allow them to guide you towards your true self and your true purpose.

Go deep into yourself to find your purpose by listing your professional attributes and inclinations.

- Our drifts tend to emerge when the mind is still, so try choosing a quiet day to meditate or practice relaxation techniques. Notice activities that cause you to slip into a state of flow, as these often point us toward our drifts.
- Consider which activities you possess a natural aptitude or talent for, perhaps using a strengths-finding exercise. You may give them a score based on strengths and weaknesses on a scale of one to ten.
- Think about which activities you find intrinsically motivating. These are the activities you would undertake without external rewards, such as money or the approval of others.
- Notice times when you feel a strong sense of personal responsibility to do something or have a unique vision about how something should be carried out.
- What would you pursue even after being discouraged by observers?

Personal Principles

To understand ourselves better, we should begin by identifying the principles or core beliefs that matter most to us. These core beliefs define who we are. It's essential that our principles stay consistent as we work; otherwise, we might struggle to feel happy and fulfilled in what we do. The fundamental attributes discussed in the previous chapter serve as our foundation.

We should identify the top four tenets or principles that are most important to us. They could be Integrity, Excellence, Respect, Achievement, Customer value, Honesty, Loyalty, Freedom, Fairness, diversity, Altruism and Accountability.

Also, add principles related to leadership, like Empathy and Relationships

My top four are: Integrity, Fairness, Freedom and Leadership.

Once you have these principles prioritised, define what they mean to you. People can have different interpretations of it, so be clear about what they mean to you. Values and principles are the foundation of your character.

For me, they would mean:

Integrity: Presenting ethical behaviour and doing the right thing all the time. Here, the right thing to do is to perform our role as per set norms.

Fairness: Treating people without discrimination of any kind. This does not always mean they will be treated equally. Equality involves treating everyone exactly the same. Understanding fairness and equality goes hand-in-hand with increasing tolerance and appreciation for diverse learners.

Freedom: It means having the right to think, act, and speak as one chooses without limitations or restrictions. Being coerced to behave in a way that differs from your true self is not real freedom.

Leadership: Having the compassion to understand people and support them appropriately. Respecting every individual and always keeping relationships on a high pedestal.

These principles are essential to me because they help maintain my self-image.

Once you recognize your core principles and understand the essence of your character, the next step is to align these principles with those of your workplace. Understanding your core values helps you apply them effectively in your daily life.

For example, if someone values Integrity as a core driving principle in their life, he will never feel comfortable if he is made to compromise it. Understanding it with an example.

You were asked to provide daily progress reports for a critical project. After you highlighted a quality inspection concern, your manager asked you to revise the report and downplay the issue as insignificant, as highlighting it would delay the project. However, as per the approved procedure, it could lead to safety issues later. When 'Integrity' is considered as one of the guiding principles, the available choices are: 1. Requesting a suitable amendment of the quality inspection procedure, stating how to deal with such issues. 2. Seeking deviation approval for the procedure. 3. Requesting a mail from the manager to make amendments to the report or suggesting an alternative way of reporting the deviation. If it is believed that none of these steps would be effective and raising a flag would have negative repercussions due to the company's lack of a fair policy to address such incidents, it should be acknowledged that personal principles may not align with the company's principles.

Driving Attributes for Profession

At this stage, we will take the time to carefully identify and articulate the professional attributes that most accurately reflect our skills, values, and strengths. These attributes will help us understand how to contribute effectively in our roles and define our unique professional identities.

Go through the list given below to find the most suitable professional attributes that may align with you:

Family happiness, health, competitiveness, mediation, helping others, personal development, love of country, recognition, love for nature, status, spirituality, religion, adventure, teaching, acting, economic security, pleasure, fame, achievement, wealth, hospitality, power, stability, creativity, attention to detail, problem-solving, logical thinking, analytical skills, ethnicity, political activism, teamwork, organization, social justice, physical appearance, excitement, physical labour, critical thinking, fixing things, writing, speaking, playing and research.

Also, attributes related to leadership, such as communication, conflict resolution, and networking, should be added.

You may further add to this list if I have missed out on your favourites.

From the list, choose the attributes that suit you best. Then, prioritise by reducing it to half, then half again. Follow the process until you have the top three.

You can count leadership as one attribute.

My top three are: Helping others, Leadership and Creativity

Once you have sorted the three attributes, describe each in your own words. What do they mean to you?

I would describe my three attributes as follows;

Helping others: It involves understanding people's needs, guiding them to lead a life of their choice, and helping them fulfil their objectives. It also comprises assisting people in overcoming stress and building a meaningful and happy life.

Leadership: Underlying principles that positively influence my ability to help, guide, take support and lead the community I interact with.

Creativity: I believe that I can achieve my goals in different interesting ways. I work to understand and connect with ideas that are outside my usual thinking. I choose the best methods to complete new tasks and meet people's needs more effectively.

My goals, and likewise your goals, will originate from these seven definitions. They will serve as the guiding light on your journey from now on. We can decide how to showcase them through our strengths by selecting the right career.

It is also essential to identify the required skills and determine what kind of upskilling is required to enhance our strengths and address our weaknesses.

I once asked a girl who works as a supply chain executive in a company, "What do you like to do in your free time to boost your energy?" She replied, "I love painting." I asked, "Does that help you in any way?" She said, "It's my hobby, and it helps me relax and find inner joy. I have also won several painting competitions in my school days. But since I work full-time, I don't get enough time to pursue it." I then asked her if she liked painting more than her job, and she said, "Yes, my job gives me a lot of stress." I asked, "Why is it so?" She said, "Haven't you done a job? Jobs are always stressful. We do it to run our family." I said—"Yeah, okay. But can't you pursue painting as a career?" She said, "Who will feed my family then?"

Most of us think in the same manner. Either we lack the courage to adopt the work we love as our profession, or we lack the imagination to do it on a scale to make a living out of it. Our goals and pathways to achieve them are limited by what we see in our surroundings. Very few of us take our work as something to be enjoyed every day. And, when we see somebody making a good business out of their work, we fleetingly remark it to be a matter of luck or chance. We never go beyond that to find out why the person succeeded.

We don't devote time to what we like most and drag through most parts of our lives to earn a living or to live up to society's expectations. Now, ask yourself, can you excel in your work with this attitude? It is said, "Work is worship." If our work is not giving us joy, how can we worship it?

The question in the previous example is whether a hobby can lead to a fulfilling career. Research indicates that it is possible, particularly if there is a strong commitment to the hobby and adequate preparation. If there is hesitation, it may stem from a lack of a clear vision for transitioning a passion into a career. The current job market offers numerous opportunities. For instance, a painter or artist may collaborate with an interior designer to provide artwork in specialized areas such as corporate offices, hotels, airport lobbies, and other public spaces. Successful execution of such collaborations often requires leadership and relationship-building skills.

One way of being creative is when you apply the learning of one subject or field to your other field of work, especially in your profession. Steve Jobs, founder of Apple Inc., said that when he had nothing to do, he learned calligraphy, which is decorative handwriting. Years later, he applied this knowledge while designing Macintosh- Apple's first successful personal computer with a graphical user interface. Introducing calligraphy into computers has led to the art of beautiful letter writing thriving worldwide in thousands of ways. Also, though Mr Jobs was certainly hooked on the creativity of calligraphy, there were additional creative foundational elements the class instilled in him that helped him in his chosen business. The design and aesthetics of Apple products were valued equally as the functionality.

When you work on something you love, your mind works creatively and produces many ideas.

Your creative brain gets free rein when you love your work.

Raaj Sinha

Ensure that the selected attributes reflect your deep-down desires and willingness to perform these roles without inhibitions. While choosing the attributes, be clear that they represent your inner core in some way, and they should not just be your aspirations. Be honest with yourself. For example, a person may aspire to be a very good dancer (creative art form) but may lack the basic knack for it, like discipline, patience and physical strength. Similarly, to become an engineer, one should have good logical and analytical reasoning, attention to detail, problem-solving, and technical and communication skills. One should avoid picking up goals that do not fit in with one's attributes.

When you find yourself, don't hold back. Respect what comes from within and encourage yourself to explore your mind fully. Every discovery should prompt questions, and we must seek answers to those questions. These answers may lead to more questions and answers.

Example:

“I love to invest in companies' stocks.”

Question: Why do you love to do that?

Answer: It can make you rich quickly.

Question: What is your experience? How do you select stocks? What is your CAGR return in a bear market?

Answer: More than three years of experience. I read news and listen to experts and tips from reliable sources. It is not calculated, but it is difficult to make a return in a bear market.

Question: “How many hours do you give to the stock market?”

Answer: “One to two hours, but not regular.”

Thought: You are similar to many others who invest in stocks without fully understanding the companies involved. After three years, you still haven't shared any meaningful insights. If you genuinely care about something, you should monitor your progress, recall what you’ve learned, show creativity, and adapt to challenging situations.

Another Example:

“I love exploring food from different varieties and cultures.”

Question: “What’s so great about it?”

Answer: "That's just who I am. I constantly seek opportunities to visit new places and try different foods."

Question: "Many people enjoy this; what makes it different for you?"

Answer: "If I discover a dish I like, I often attempt to make it myself. I enjoy being creative in the kitchen and experimenting with various ingredient combinations."

Question: "Can you tell me more about your food preparation process?"

Answer: "Seeing the delighted faces of people when they taste my food brings me joy. I also welcome feedback positively and use it to keep experimenting. I love telling others about my recipes. While preparing meals, I feel fully accountable for the outcome. I believe I'm spreading love through the dishes I make."

Question: "How much time can you spend in the kitchen each day?"

Answer: "I can spend a significant amount of time in the kitchen, either preparing food myself or guiding others in the cooking process."

Thought: From your explanations, it is clear that you hold a passion for the art of cooking.

No work is small or big. It is our thinking that makes it look small or big. It always helps to encourage or applaud others when they exhibit their talent. As Oprah Winfrey said in one of her interviews, "Everybody has talent. But when you see others' talent and become envious of it, you are putting it in a negative way inside you, and it goes away from you."

You have to focus on what you have to offer. What can you give? How can you be used in service? Not everybody can become famous. But everybody can become great because greatness is determined by service. Whatever job you choose can be switched to become more fulfilling. Whatever job you like, you have to think about how I service to put it as something bigger than myself. If you think this way, it no longer becomes a job but an offering to this world.

People who started as tailors or cobblers with a vision to serve society in a genuine way and apply creativity skilfully have grown their businesses multiple-fold. Their products are sold in every corner of the world.

Jacob Davis was a tailor in Nevada, US; He got a unique way of stitching pants for mining workers. At the point of strain, he used to put rivets to make the pants last longer. This idea was patented with the help of a cloth wholesale merchant, Mr Levi Strauss, and Levi's brand came into existence.

Tomas, Anna, and Antonin were from a cobbler family. They started with a small shoe shop in Zlin, Czechoslovakia. Their innovative shoe style soon became popular. Within three years, they started producing in batches, brought in machines, and rapidly spread to several other countries. Now, they are in 155 countries. We are talking about Bata, the shoe company.

Every business starts with a thought, and then creative and innovative thinking takes it to great heights step by step.

The key is to discover yourself first.

"If you want to enjoy Life, discover yourself first."

Raaj Sinha

Remember two things:

1. Only a few people will understand the true meaning of life and be determined to realize their dreams. The rest will leave the planet one day, having just led a mediocre life. The biggest motivator for extraordinary people is how they would like to be remembered after they die. Therefore, while living, they build their legacy.
2. The greatest motivation one gets in life is by helping others.

Motivation in life can come from any time and in any form. Let's go through this incident.

A short incident…

One morning in 1888, a man was reading a newspaper when suddenly he saw a "condolence message." He was stunned to see it because it had his name on it, as the deceased person.

He was shocked to read his name. He couldn't believe that instead of reporting his brother Ludwig's death, the newspaper had reported him to be dead. He went still for a few moments! Then he somehow came back to his senses and thought, let's see how people have reacted to my death.

He started reading...it said in French, "The Merchant of Death is dead."

This was an even bigger blow for him. He thought, "Is this how I'll be remembered when I'm gone?"

That day brought a revolutionary change to his life. From that day on, this dynamite inventor began working for world peace and social welfare. Before dying, he donated his immovable property to reward those who do excellent work in science and social welfare.

The name of that great person was Alfred Bernhard Nobel, and today, it is in his name that the "Nobel Prize" is awarded every year. Now, no one remembers him as a "merchant of death" but as a great scientist and social worker.

The power of dynamite can break rocks, but the power of our thoughts can break all barriers between us and society. It is from our everyday thoughts that we create our destiny. **Regulate your thoughts to find inner clarity and stability.**

Sometimes, people experience a moment of realisation or awakening that motivates them to change their career path, even after many years in their current jobs. It happened to me as well. In such a situation, it is crucial to plan and prepare for the transition and embrace the new challenge instead of dwelling on past regrets. Overcoming the fear of stepping into the unknown is often a major concern for those seeking change.

To become better, one must leave today's so-called good life.

To avoid the feeling of not living life to the fullest, it is important to keep an open mind, be aware of the inner calling that one may experience, and find opportunities that may have come close to you.

Self-awareness is a fundamental tool for self-discovery.

If required, go through the chapter again and answer the "Find yourself" questionnaire.

Note: Give yourself just 1 minute to think for each question.

'Find yourself' Questionnaire:

1. What are your best qualities/characteristics?

____

____

____

2. What behaviours, traits, or qualities do you want others to admire in you?

____

____

____

3. What are the three most important Values to you?

____

____

____

4. Who are the people with whom you feel 'yourself'?

____

____

____

5. Which of your talents or skills gives you the greatest sense of pride or satisfaction?

6. What talents or skills do you admire most in others?

7. What are your five greatest strengths?

Chapter 22
Building the Image core: Setting your Goals

Establishing clear and meaningful goals is vital in our lives. Our objectives shape our actions and significantly influence our long-term identity and achievements. We create a blueprint for personal and professional growth by setting specific goals. These goals reflect our values and aspirations, ultimately defining who we will become and how we navigate future challenges and opportunities.

The previous chapters have provided us with clarity about the self, and now it is time to take action to achieve a higher sense of self. By developing a positive self-image and discovering your true attributes, you will be able to set meaningful goals. These goals can significantly transform your life, evolving into your dreams. Ensure that these dreams become the greatest influence on your daily decisions and activities. They will be the greatest pull on you.

Quote from Swami Vivekananda the youth icon of the century for India.

"Life itself has no meaning; it is an opportunity to create meaning."

Swami Vivekananda

Your principles can guide you in deciding with whom you want to work or what kind of working culture you will gel with, while your attributes can help you determine the profession that would suit you best. This holds for both businessmen and job professionals.

Also, when choosing a career, it's important to be aware of changing technologies, preferences, cultures, demands, and behaviour patterns worldwide.

For example, the demand for core engineering skills has decreased nowadays. This is due to the emergence of proven software tools that apply artificial intelligence and machine learning. Software tools are now more efficient in collecting and analysing system-related data, reducing the need for human involvement in these tasks. AI is also being utilised to improve systems' functionality, performance, and predictability, resulting in less costly downtime.

Choosing a career must be done wisely. It should neither be something that is becoming obsolete or holds less value, nor be overly crowded, meaning many people compete for the same opportunity.

AI will affect jobs related to data gathering and data entry, telemarketers, factory workers performing repetitive jobs, bank tellers, customer service, market research analysts, etc.

Do not choose a career that doesn’t provide financial stability. Many jobs that were once highly valued have become obsolete due to technological advancements and automation. Similarly, various degrees and professions have lost their significance over time. Avoid falling into the trap of pursuing trendy degrees that may not have long-term value.

It is essential to evaluate the worth of a degree or profession based on current and evolving societal needs before making a decision. A person should take pride in their work, as it fosters a sense of fulfilment and satisfaction. However, it’s easy to overlook the financial viability of a job while seeking personal meaning. It's important to align your understanding of a meaningful life with the financial resources required to sustain that life. Ultimately, earning money is necessary for living.

The job market is in a state of constant evolution, significantly shaped by technological advancements. Skills and knowledge that are valued today may shift in importance tomorrow. For instance, two decades ago, the introduction of computers transformed business operations. In the present day, smartphones have emerged as a critical factor influencing a variety of industries. To remain competitive, it has become imperative for businesses to develop mobile applications that effectively serve their customers' needs.

Regularly reviewing your goals is essential for ongoing personal and professional development. As circumstances, locations, and societal needs evolve, our objectives must adapt accordingly. However, striking a balance is crucial; frequent and excessive changes can diminish your market value. To maintain high worth in your chosen field, focus on innovating systems, processes, or products that resonate with your expertise. This approach will ensure that your goals remain relevant while enhancing your impact.

A few important points:

- Do the due diligence to understand which business or job suits you. Just do not copy others.
- Innovate yourself in your chosen profession.
- Goals should be set with a high spirit and enjoyable to achieve.
- Set short-term and long-term goals.

- From a risk-reward perspective, give the required weightage to critical actions for achieving your goals.
- Don't choose a complicated goal. Start with simple and easy-to-achieve things.

Let's consider an example that we often overlook. It involves how a simple taxi driver innovates and delights his customers.

Duck or Eagle

I was waiting in line for a ride from the airport in Delhi, India. When a cab pulled up, the first thing I noticed was that the taxi was polished to a bright shine. Smartly dressed in a white shirt, black tie, and freshly pressed black slacks, the cab driver jumped out and rounded the car to open the back passenger door for me. He handed me a laminated card and said, "I'm Anirudh, your driver. While I'm loading your bags in the trunk, I'd like you to read my mission statement."

Taken aback, I read the card. It said -

Anirudh's Mission Statement:

To get my customers to their destination in the quickest, safest and cheapest way possible in a friendly environment.

This blew me away, especially when I noticed that the inside of the cab matched the outside—it was spotlessly clean!

As he slid behind the wheel, Anirudh asked, "Would you like a cup of coffee? I have a regular thermos and one that is decaf."

I replied jokingly, "No, I'd prefer a soft drink."

Anirudh smiled and said, "No problem. I have a cooler up front with regular and Diet Coke, lassi, water and orange juice."

Almost stuttering, I said, "I'll take a Lassi."

Handing me my drink, Anirudh said, “If you'd like something to read, I have The Times of India, the Hindustan Times, and Indian Express with me today.”

As traffic pulled away, Anirudh handed me another laminated card, "These are the stations I get and the music they play if you'd like to listen to the radio."

As if that weren't enough, Anirudh told me he had the air conditioning on and asked if the temperature was comfortable.

Then he advised me of the best route to my destination for that time of day. He also told me he'd be happy to chat and tell me about some of the sights or, if I preferred, to leave me with my thoughts.

"Tell me, Aniruddh," I was amazed and asked him, "Have you always served customers like this?"

Anirudh smiled into the rear-view mirror. "No, not always. It's only been in the last two years. During my first five years driving, I spent most of my time complaining like all the rest of the cabbies do. Then I heard about ‘the power of choice’ one day.

The power of choice is that you can be either a duck or an eagle.

If you get up in the morning expecting to have a bad day, you'll rarely disappoint yourself. Stop complaining!"

He paused and then continued.

'Don't be a duck. Be an eagle. Ducks quack and complain. Eagles soar above the crowd.'

"That hit me really hard,” said Anirudh.

"It is about me. I was always quacking and complaining, so I changed my attitude and became an eagle. I looked around at the other cabs and their drivers. The cabs were dirty, the drivers were unfriendly, and the customers were unhappy. So, I decided to make some changes, slowly, a few at a time. When my customers responded well, I did more."

"I take it that it has paid off for you," I said.

"It sure has," Anirudh replied with a smile. "My first year as an eagle, I doubled my income from the previous year. This year, I'll probably quadruple it. My customers call me for appointments on my cell phone or leave a message on it."

How many such taxis do we see on Indian roads? Why do most of the taxis present a shabby look? Why do most of the taxi drivers seem to be worked up or stuck in their jobs?

Anirudh made a different choice. He decided to stop quacking like a duck and start soaring like an eagle. He understood that once you have chosen a career, you need to do it magnificently to delight your customers. And the rest is taken care of.

Many accumulate wealth but still feel unhappy in the end. This is because what they were doing was not closely connected to their hearts. Even though they may give the impression of being content, deep inside, they know they have ignored their inner voice. Without self-awareness, it isn't easy to hear your inner voice, and you may spend your entire life without a clear purpose, wandering aimlessly in a maze by copying others. I think that's a life that is not well lived.

Your goal should be aligned with your purpose in life. It should also be aligned with your core values. You should have a clear picture of what kind of job suits the personality you are or have decided to become. Who do you want to work with? Where do you want to live? Who do you want to befriend? Who do you want to help or serve? What skills do you have? What skills do you need to upgrade now to get to the desired level?

Your service to society should have the combination of your passion, your skill and its demand in the market. Your mojo.

The diagram to show this...

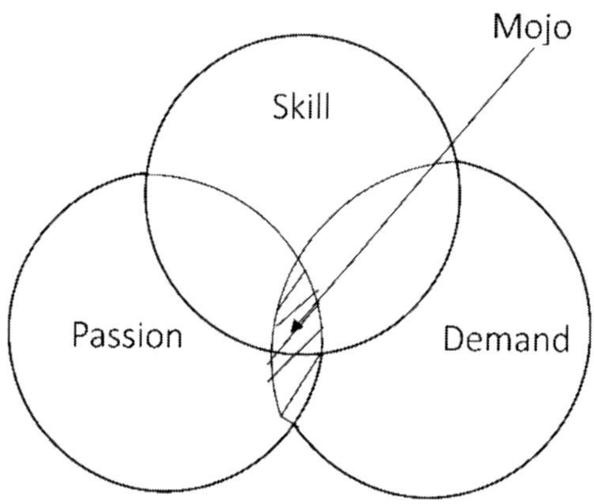

Career Selection

[Fig 8]

You need to have a 'strong and clear' understanding of why you would be doing that job, business or being associated with it. This 'why' should be the guiding force for offering your products or services to society. It provides you with the constant pull to stick to your goals.

The most fulfilling goal is to meet both your intrinsic and extrinsic needs. Intrinsic needs are based on your values and core beliefs, which you should never compromise. While pursuing your goals, it's also essential to meet your emotional, behavioural, and relational needs. This approach will lead you to a life without compromise and help you maintain a high self-image. By doing so, you can experience true fulfilment and happiness.

When I talk to children and young adults about their aspirations, I often hear some expressing a desire to earn a significant income or choose careers for the financial rewards. Others convey that they prefer a simple, peaceful life without the need for extraordinary achievements. While these viewpoints reflect their current understanding, they present an opportunity for guidance toward discovering their true passions and potential. To lead a fulfilling life, it is important to seek out a meaningful purpose. Finding meaning can illuminate our path and help us embrace our unique contributions. With a clear sense of purpose, life can become vibrant and inspiring.

If your primary focus in life is on making money, it's important to recognize that this mindset can sometimes create a sense of disconnect. When core values are not fulfilled, true happiness may feel elusive. Engaging in work solely for financial gain can lead to a reliance on the "carrot and stick" approach, which may prevent you from finding genuine enjoyment in your job. This can ultimately impact your overall quality of life, potentially leading to feelings of anxiety.

To foster a stronger sense of belonging and fulfilment in your professional life, it's essential to explore work that aligns with your values and passions. By prioritising meaningful contributions and nurturing a genuine connection to your work, you can enhance your overall well-being and create a more fulfilling career path over time.

If you allow your passion to guide you, you will discover true fulfilment and long-term happiness. Your job should enable you to pursue your passion, with financial rewards being a by-product of your efforts rather than the primary purpose of your life.

Some may argue that money is the greatest motivator. To them, I would say all the inventors, philosophers, socialists, teachers, and even your parents who brought you up with patience and dedication were not all for money but for the love of what they do. Many people make the mistake of aimlessly chasing money, ending up feeling unfulfilled and unhappy.

The other group of youths who claim that they do not aspire to do anything extraordinary are the ones who are attempting to avoid the pressure that has been placed upon them by society. They have yet to understand their purpose in life and want to avoid the conundrum they see in their surroundings. They have been living to meet society's expectations and not their own. Sadly, many parents are unaware of how to handle such a situation, and they say, "Don't worry about the pressure; we have enough to get by." However, they fail to realize that if they give up on striving for success, they will eventually find themselves in a state of inaction and stagnation. No one can lead a happy life without doing something meaningful. We are designed to lead successful lives by setting goals and achieving them. It is up to us to decide what goals we want to set for ourselves.

A responsible individual strives to contribute positively to society, or at the very least, to their family. This contribution can have a meaningful impact on the lives of others. Engaging actively in community activities is far more fulfilling than merely observing from the sidelines. To make the most of your involvement, set ambitious goals and work to continuously surpass them, fostering both personal growth and a greater benefit to those around you.

Exercise:

1. Do you feel delighted for your job? How do you reflect your pride in the job?

   ____

   ____

   ____

2. If the Answer to question 1 is 'No', list the reasons for which you feel let down.

   ____

   ____

   ____

3. What are the aspects that you should have in mind while making a job selection?

   ____

   ____

   ____

4. Why money cannot be the prime reason for job selection?

   ____

   ____

   ____

Set big Goals

We are often reminded to set smaller goals. This is because lofty targets can lead to feeling over-pressurized before even starting. While this advice is correct, it does not explain the importance of speed in achieving our targets. Setting smaller goals is just a part of the process. The speed at which you reach your target depends on how ambitious your goals are.

I would like to mention the quote of the legendary Indian businessman, Sh. Dhirubhai Ambani, probably one of the greatest rags-to-riches stories in India.

"Dream big, dream fast, ideas are no one's monopoly."

Dreaming big speeds up the entire process of thinking, planning and executing.

The first step in achieving our goals is to build endurance. This process may not be as fast as one may think, but it certainly has to be continuous and should go along with your progress towards your goals in life. I have discussed endurance in the bonus section.

One can pick up some clues while setting targets for goals by going through the journey of successful and progressive individuals in their chosen field. Top achievers typically follow the principle of setting highly ambitious goals and taking massive action to achieve them. By doing so, they make steady progress towards their goals at a good pace.

You would also agree that achieving something memorable requires sincere, relentless effort. This can be related to when you recall any of your achievements in the past.

Remember, your high self-image is built upon a foundation of good character, intelligence, and a focus on aligning your thoughts and processes towards your goal. With barriers removed, these attributes provide a strong base for your personality and have simplified your thoughts, allowing you to reach greater heights in your chosen way of serving society.

In his book "The 10X Rule," Grant Cardone emphasizes the importance of putting in ten times the effort that others do in order to achieve success. To reach your goals, it's crucial to have abundant energy and enthusiasm. While you may encounter unexpected obstacles along the way, don't let them discourage you. Celebrate every small accomplishment and use that feeling of success to stay motivated. It's also important to continue increasing your targets, as growth is essential for long-term success. If you're not moving forward, you risk falling behind.

List down your goals. Define their objectives. Define relevance. Define resources required. Define timelines.

The goal we have established for ourselves would require certain basic traits to achieve it. List down the skills and the level of proficiency needed vis-à-vis how you rate yourself at present. The attributes can be on physical, mental and emotional levels. What kind of physical fitness do you require? What should be your level of calm and composed attitude? How do you apply your fundamental attitudes and principles to remain focused and energized daily? If you are a student, you can imagine improving your memory and learning ability. List them all on paper. Work on each one of them separately. It is all about imagining the character you would like to manifest into.

Setting and pursuing goals can significantly shape and enhance your personality. This transformation is one of the most valuable benefits you can gift yourself.

In the corporate world, it is commonly advised to set SMART goals. SMART stands for Specific, Measurable, Attainable, Relevant, and Time-bound. It is crucial to divide your significant goals into smaller ones and then break them down further into daily tasks. It is important to understand that achieving your big goal requires consistency and hard work, as there are no overnight successes. Therefore, staying focused and committed throughout the process is essential.

Specific	Define what is expected as an end result clearly. Detail the process with the exact level of effort required. Example- If the goal is to improve the overall look. One specific goal can be reducing body weight.
Measurable	Identify how you will know that objectives have been achieved. It can be quantity or quality, or both can be defined here. For example, “I want to be an excellent blog writer” could be better written as “I would become a top-class blog writer with 1 million followers within 2 years.” Or, for the above example, reduce the weight by 5 kg.
Attainable	Do not give a timeline that is not achievable. A timeline of 14 days to reduce

	5 kg from a 70 kg body may strain you, and results may not be long-lasting, especially if you have never exercised or followed a weight loss regime
Relevant	Is the Goal aligned with your core ideology, values, skills and passion? *Note: The business perspective may change to remain relevant with changing times, but the core ideology should remain the same.* How will weight reduction help you achieve your ultimate goal? Also, keep checking your daily tasks to see how relevant they are to your goals.
Time Bound	Specify when the objective should be accomplished—a clearly defined end date. Example: a drop of 2 kg in one week and thereafter 1 kg every week. Include timeline benchmarks for your goals so that you do not take longer than a reasonable time to get to your result.

Be action-oriented and focused on your goals. Once we establish our goals, they become integral to our daily lives. Write your goals clearly every morning and assess your progress every night. You will notice that you become more focused on your goals each day. This routine will help you achieve clarity and bring you closer to your goals. Make it a part of your *daily journal.*

Energy and excitement are vital for high performance. A clear purpose boosts mental energy and enthusiasm. Setting and achieving daily goals can increase our energy levels; a well-defined purpose helps sustain this energy.

Exercise

1. Why should you set big goals?

   ____

   ____

   ____

2. How to set meaningful goals?

   ____

   ____

   ____

Chapter 23
Building the Image Core: Forming Structures

Once you have set goals that fulfil your purpose and harmonise with your principles and attributes, you must build patterns in your image core to have a focused approach.

We internalise them through a process. Deep faith in ourselves and commitment to the process will build the core structure of our self-image.

Visualise your goals

Visualisation is a powerful technique for achieving set goals. Whether it is your daily tasks or broader life goals, it is an excellent practice to visualize them every day. It is about creating a clear mental picture of ideas, feelings, or objects to attain our goals.

The technique is used to program our brain to see our goals and activate the creative potential of our brain to understand the resources required to achieve the goal. Then, build the resources to see yourself vividly, achieving your goals.

We know that the brain perceives pictures as strong signals. Therefore, it is said that "a picture is worth a thousand words." Through visualization techniques, we imagine vivid pictures that help repeatedly transmit strong signals to the core to form impressions.

Before starting any task, imagining it in our minds is essential. The likelihood of success in a particular task depends on how clearly we can visualize the process and the outcome before even attempting it. Visualization of the ultimate outcome keeps us motivated towards achieving our goal. For instance, if the goal is to have a fit body, imagine yourself as a person with a fit body who can run a marathon, row a boat, swim long distances, and impress your partner. By the way, receiving compliments from others can also serve as great motivation.

When we do this with required emotions, the deeper section of our brain, i.e. the core, receives signals to form the patterns aligned with our imagination. Once these patterns form in our self-image, they attract more such signals, and our imagination becomes more vivid.

Imagining our goals helps us understand the necessary actions to achieve them. However, many individuals face challenges in effective planning due to a lack of confidence in their thinking abilities. Fortunately, this perception can be transformed. By adopting a clear self-image that doesn't have mental barriers and complexities, individuals can find that their minds can plan with greater freedom and effectiveness.

A positive self-image provides us with the confidence of a winner. While building a positive self-image, we often use our imagination and positive affirmations to develop the desired personality traits. By maintaining appropriate behaviour in our day-to-day lives, we can stay focused on our goals and not waste time on things of little or no value to us.

Focus on the outcome:

Envision yourself as a role model in your chosen field and list the behavioural traits and actions this model would display as part of their character.

To fully embody this new character, we must begin to live as if we are already the person we aspire to be. This empowers us to bring our envisioned future selves into the present and believe that we are already living the life of our dream character. As a result, we take responsibility for presenting our behaviour in a manner that aligns with our idealized self-concept.

Making outcomes a reality from the beginning is an easy-to-understand and focused approach to what we desire. It gives us the necessary push to create and continue with the new habit.

There is no better feeling than the feeling of becoming an Achiever.

The driving force behind achieving your goals comes from a deep sense of responsibility to live the life you desire. It's about embodying your dreams in the present moment. This involves taking action with total commitment, as knowing that others are observing you holds you accountable and fosters sincerity. Being prepared means being ready to take responsibility for your actions. This is how the power of belief propels you on the fast track to achievement.

We strongly desire to adopt habits that help us improve and achieve our objectives, whether it's having a calm and alert mind, getting in shape, building or improving a relationship, learning music, becoming prosperous, serving a community, etc.

However, it's essential to understand why we want to achieve them. For example, when it comes to getting in shape, people often lose motivation after a while, making it difficult to carry on. Other priorities take the lead, and one may feel it is painful or not fruitful to continue with. We often see people grooming themselves before marriage, but once they are married, they let their fitness routines fall by the wayside. Students study hard as the exam nears, and the same old routine sets in once it's over. Short-term goals are easily achieved but are quickly forgotten. Your priorities keep changing, and so do your actions, which finally affects the process. This has happened because your self-image receives weak signals for these activities. Such signals find it difficult to reach the core and drop off from the subconscious mind after some time. Changing your self-image to one with fitness at its core is the key to a lifelong fitness habit. While building your Image core, it's crucial to have a clearly defined bold fitness pattern/objective that generates a strong signal for maintaining a fit and healthy body and mind. Such a person will have a perpetual momentum to pursue their fitness goals.

When the idea or a thought to improve oneself doesn't have a compelling reason, the changes don't happen in the core of our self-image. *Without a strong signal from the image core, procrastination and indecision take root in one's character.* No focused approach results in a waste of time and effort with no significant result.

Now imagine your goal is to become the winner of a beauty pageant or a personality contest, which everybody will be looking at in magazines and TV shows. People want to take a photo with you. Imagine it, and you declare within yourself that you are already the winner of the beauty pageant and that you are a celebrity. Your behaviour and your actions will change. You cannot afford to have a body that is out of shape. People are already looking at you like a celebrity. You cannot go in hiding. Your every move is being watched. You are a role model for many. Your mind continuously signals for actions to reach your goal or the outcome. The whole process is driven from inwards. Driven from the core of a reconstructed self-image.

In today's world, every successful person wants a physically fit body and mentally fit mind to operate at a high level. Therefore, habits relating to fitness are becoming a norm. The drive has to come from within. And the drive should be a compelling one. If you know that you will lose your present job because you are not fit, or you may miss your next promotion, or your next business deal may not click, then come what may, you will not leave that habit, right? Read the chapters in the book several times, if required, until you acquire the SMS ring in your life. Imagine already operating at a legendary level in your chosen field. As discussed earlier, you become deeply invested in making a change when cultivating a positive self-image. You are confident in your abilities and believe you will achieve your goals.

To reach a goal, it's essential to recognize that a specific process must be followed. A process is a series of steps that must be taken in a specific order to attain the desired outcome.

Enjoy the process. Enjoy the game!

The visualization technique

Visualizing a goal can be challenging for many people, especially when starting. It may be helpful to begin by visualizing small daily tasks. Some examples may be:

Going to the gym: What exercises should be done today and in what sequence?

Preparing for attending a meeting: As per the meeting agenda, check how updated you are and see if you require any preparation.

Preparing food in the kitchen: What to prepare, getting the ingredients, how to prepare, and likewise.

Let's pick up the last one—preparing food in the kitchen.

1. [Task] Fix up the recipe in mind 2. List down the ingredients. 3. Know the process 4. Identify all the critical parts of the process and precautions to be taken. 5. See if you have all the resources to make the dish. 6. Get the ingredients 7. Make the dish 8. Taste it to check if it is made as thought initially. 9. Note points for improvements, if any.

When setting goals, it's helpful to focus on one activity at a time and visualize the entire process of that activity from beginning to end, especially for daily tasks. By identifying the challenging steps, we can determine where to focus more on those specific steps to gain clarity. When choosing a goal, start with those that seem relatively attainable. It's essential to recognize that no goals are inherently easy or difficult; some may be easier or harder to visualize, while we might lack the necessary skills to perform them.

Creating a mental image of the desired outcome can be helpful when setting a goal. For example, when preparing a dish in the kitchen, the picture of the prepared dish first comes to mind. We get to feel the look and aroma of the prepared food, which thus becomes a driving force in making that recipe.

Similarly, when working on bigger goals like transforming into a higher character, create a clear picture and the required behaviour in your mind. One has to visualize the feelings of embodying the idolized character.

To gain insight into achieving success, reading biographies or autobiographies of distinguished individuals within your field is advisable. By analyzing their journeys, one can identify significant milestones in their careers, the challenges they encountered, and the strategies they employed to overcome these obstacles. Pay attention to the specific skills and competencies that contributed to their accomplishments and enhance your understanding of these skills through relevant tutorials. However, it is crucial to avoid mere imitation, as each individual possesses unique qualities. Engaging in such imitation may result in undue stress, self-criticism, and feelings of inferiority, which can create various internal barriers.

Visualize the mental image two or three times a day. Do this in the morning and during your rest breaks throughout the day. Focus on it clearly but with ease and comfort. Avoid straining to maintain your focus.

Giving strong signals

To develop the core pattern, we must affirm the presence of those tenets within us while focusing on the envisioned outcome.

Let us understand the principle that helps develop the core patterns in the self-image.

The universe operates according to a set of unchanging laws and principles that govern its functioning. Among these is the Law of Attraction, a powerful concept that suggests that our thoughts and desires can influence the reality we experience. This law posits that when you have a deep and compelling desire to manifest something in your life, you can attract that desired outcome to yourself.

However, the effectiveness of this attraction hinges on the intensity of your desire. It's not merely wishing for something; it requires a fervent longing that permeates every aspect of your being. This means that every cell in your body should resonate with the same frequency as your desire, creating a harmonious vibration that aligns with what you seek. When your entire essence is in tune with this intention, the universe responds, reinforcing the notion that what you focus on expands. Thus, cultivating a strong and unwavering desire is essential to effectively harnessing the power of the Law of Attraction.

It's important to note that the Law of Attraction is not magic, and it doesn't work by simply wishing for things to happen. Instead, it aligns your thoughts, feelings, and actions with your desires.

When we practice affirmations daily, structures start building up in the core, and in a few weeks (3-4 weeks), we start feeling a significant change as it starts reflecting in our behaviour.

These short positive statements reprogram our minds to capture empowering beliefs, habits, and thought patterns. They help make the structure or patterns of the core of your new self-image.

Affirmations that are not life ward or positive cannot build the desired structure on the core's positive base that we have already built. Therefore, it is essential to choose your affirmations wisely.

Positive affirmations are written in the language of the brain using specific guidelines. They enter through the brain receptors and transform the core of our mind, thereby changing our self-image.

Giving consistent signals to the mind helps make impressions in the core, eventually forming the structures. As we discussed earlier, the signal must be strong to get inside and reach the core. If we remain consistent, clear, and strong in our affirmations, signals will reach the core and start building the necessary structures. This, in turn, will attract similar signals to the core. Here, a signal refers to desire, ideas, and concepts laced with emotions.

Any negative or dissimilar signals should be rejected during this process. Hence, the brain becomes accustomed to accepting only the signals necessary to build the correct core pattern. It is natural to get thoughts of doubt and disbelief at times. But you must drop such feelings immediately and move forward with your affirmations. This is discussed in the section – Being an Observer of the Mind- under the chapter Mind Control.

When the purpose is clearly defined, the signals become more explicit. When we are emotionally invested in achieving our goals, these signals become even stronger. Only clear and strong signals can create robust patterns that contribute to building a positive subconscious self. This subconscious self is aligned with our purpose.

Remember, our chosen goals should serve our purpose, and the core structure should serve our goals. Therefore, our affirmations represent our broader life goals. We need to write down our goals and transform them into affirmations.

As Dr Joseph Murphy explains in his book The Power of Subconscious Mind, "To affirm is to state that it is so. As you maintain this attitude of mind as true, regardless of all evidence to the contrary, you will receive an answer to your prayer."

Condense your affirmation into a brief phrase that can readily be recalled. Repeat it over and over again, knowing what you are saying and why you are saying it. Repeating an affirmation leads the brain receptors to transmit the signal strongly to the core.

For example, if your principles and attributes are Integrity, fairness, physical appearance, creativity, riches, etc., you can add affirmations accordingly.

- I am a highly reliable and responsible person.
- I love and admire people.
- People love and admire me.
- I am getting better every day.
- I am the master of my life.
- I am happy and prosperous.
- I am a symbol of trust and faith.
- I am the embodiment of patience and perseverance.
- I am aligned with the abundance of the universe.
- I am a blissful soul attracting positivity and vitality.
- I am a great parent to my child / I am a loving child to my parent/I am a great human being.
- I make my family and my community proud.
- I have infinite creative power.

- Creative ideas flow to me easily.
- Every day, I am growing healthier and more attractive.
- I am good to my body, and my body is good to me.
- I communicate clearly and effectively.
- This is an abundant universe, and there is plenty for all of us.
- I love doing my work, and I am richly rewarded.
- The more I give, the more I receive.
- I am God's medium to spread love and happiness.
- I am par excellence in performing my work.
- I am god's medium for creativity on this planet.
- Money flows to me easily and abundantly.

Make affirmations according to your principles, attributes, and goals. Affirm them regularly. Observe the changes in your thoughts and behaviour. Mark your progress in the daily diary.

Note: You can add affirmations relating to your field of work, visualizing yourself as an achiever in that field.

Task:

1. Make your affirmations. Write them down and place them in prominent locations where you'll be sure to see them throughout the day. This could be on your bathroom mirror, on your desk, or even on your phone lock screen. Recite these affirmations with intention and authenticity, so try to say them with your heart at least three times a day. You might also consider starting your day by reading your affirmations aloud or writing them down in a journal.
2. Journal specifically on how the affirmations went, i.e. how many times you could do it and how you are feeling each day

Exercise:

1. How does imagining yourself as a role model help? Who are the role models for you?

___

___

___

2. How can one give strong signals to the brain to form core patterns?

___

___

___

3. What actions should be taken to make the affirmation process effective?

___

___

___

Chapter 24
Building/Maintaining your self-image

Habit comes to you automatically when you start improving your self-image.

Raaj Sinha

Consistent practice is essential for acquiring the necessary skills and maintaining a positive self-image. Establishing a daily routine that incorporates time for improving and mastering these skills is essential for achieving this objective.

Mind Control

In the journey towards developing a positive self-image, we have acquired several essential skills, including fundamental attitudes, self-awareness, leadership skills, imagination, meditation, goal setting, and visualization.

Self-awareness is the starting point for building a positive self-image. Without understanding what aspects need improvement and recognizing the control we need to exert over our thoughts, true progress may remain elusive.

We have also explored fundamental attitudes and the importance of integrating them into our behaviour.

When we encounter a new task, it can often feel challenging, even if the difficulty is relatively low. This initial experience may trigger feelings of apprehension or struggle as our brains work through unfamiliar territory, trying to understand and process the new information or skills we need to acquire. However, as we practice and reinforce our purpose, our minds gradually adjust to the change.

As children, our parents and caregivers often guided us through a set of routines that shaped our daily lives. We learned the importance of personal hygiene, starting with the simple yet crucial practice of brushing our teeth each morning and night. Each day, we were reminded to take a bath, reinforcing the idea that cleanliness is vital not just for appearance but also for health.

Additionally, our meals were structured around three main meals a day—breakfast, lunch, and dinner—each designed to provide us with the necessary nutrition to grow and thrive. We were also encouraged to dedicate time to our studies, understanding that education was key to our future success.

Before going to bed, we cultivated the practice of prayer or reflection, which helped us wind down and gain a sense of peace at the end of the day. Though initially may have felt burdensome or restrictive, these routines provided a framework for our development.

As we grew older, we faced new expectations. We were encouraged to further our education, find gainful employment, and, for many of us, consider starting a family. These responsibilities could seem overwhelming, especially at first, as they demanded significant effort and commitment.

However, over time, we began to understand the importance of these daily tasks and responsibilities. We realized that they were not just chores but essential practices that contributed to balanced and healthy living. Gradually, these routines became ingrained in our subconscious minds, making us feel more at ease in managing our daily lives. What once seemed daunting transformed into a comfortable rhythm that supports our well-being.

Similarly, we need to practice the required skills regularly to acquire fundamental attitudes and maintain focus on our daily goals. We will learn to correct our thoughts, behaviours, and actions by applying tools that have helped me and many others live the desired life and make it a part of our daily routine.

Being an observer of the Mind

Focus on structuring your core to prioritize what is most important to you and drop everything that doesn't align with your values and purpose. This will allow you to build a core that focuses on the time, energy, and resources that enrich your life rather than getting caught up in issues that won't matter to you in the long run.

An observer's mind is separate from our normal logical thinking mind; it is pure, not influenced by emotions, and so is rational and impartial. Like a good instructor, when the mind deviates from the charted-out path, our observer mind gently guides us to the required path. The observer mind is always dispassionate and focused towards making our mind fully aware and guiding us to live in the present moment. The observer mind does not focus on the outcome but just the process.

Recognizing that each of us possesses an observer's mind—an innate purity present from birth—can evoke a profound sense of reassurance. This understanding instils confidence in our journey to shape our self-image and adopt essential attitudes. It serves as a reminder that amidst life's complexities, there lies a fundamental clarity within us all, guiding our perceptions and influencing our growth. Staying alert and engaged with your surroundings is essential for a successful and fulfilling day. Be mindful of your thoughts and actively reject any negative or self-limiting beliefs that may arise. This includes being discerning about the people and environments you choose to engage with and steer clear of individuals or groups that radiate negativity or pessimism.

Additionally, be cautious of suggestions or statements from others that might disrupt your focus or hinder your advancement. It's essential to establish boundaries to protect your mental space. Instead, concentrate intently on your tasks and immerse yourself in activities that foster positivity and growth.

Your mindset plays a crucial role in shaping your reality, so consistently feed your brain with uplifting and constructive thoughts. Cultivating an environment rich in positive energy will uplift your spirits and manifest favourable outcomes in your endeavours. Surround yourself with positivity—whether through supportive relationships, inspiring content, or uplifting environments—as this will reinforce your motivation and drive throughout the day.

How to practice being an observer

Letting go of our old patterns is essential to adopt a new behaviour that reflects our core beliefs. Our previous behaviour may have been influenced by negative emotions such as anger, irritation, jealousy, self-centeredness, dislike, and hatred.

These reactions were often automatic responses to specific situations rather than deliberate actions.

Have you ever experienced a situation where a comment from a colleague, friend, parent, or spouse triggered negative emotions within you? Despite trying to control your emotions, you may have found it challenging to do so.

When working on improving your self-image, you must be aware of how negative behaviour can affect your progress. Engaging in negative behaviour should be seen as a 'Red zone alert' as it might hinder the self-image transformation process.

Managing unwarranted negative emotional behaviour is slightly trickier, as the mind has built strong connections with thoughts and logic that trigger such behaviour. During meditation, we visualize shedding such mind complexities. Use the ‘Let Go' process every day to clean up your mind. As you clear your old patterns, imagine your base ready to be built up with positive signals.

However, while building new patterns, you will encounter your previous patterns that will still affect you to some extent. This happens because memory cannot be erased completely. But as you attract and build new structures, they will attract new energies, and the old ones will gradually fade and become non-existent.

Keep in mind: Undisturbed calmness of mind is attained by cultivating:

a. Friendliness towards the happy
b. Compassion for the unhappy
c. Delight in the good
d. Indifferent to the evil or bad

Stick this at a place to remind you during your work throughout the day

During the transformation process, we must exercise restraint on our mind whenever it tries to deviate from its laid-out path. Becoming aware of our observer mind will guide us to stay on the right track.

Applying Momentus

The observer mind is the pure mind, which also represents the original self. It will now act as a master to train your impure mind to become pure.

Picture yourself behind the wheel of a car, cruising down the road. Suddenly, you notice an object approaching you from the opposite direction, threatening to collide with your vehicle. Your instinctive response is quickly hitting the brakes and steering your car away from the incoming danger. This act of swift and decisive action, which can save you from a potential accident, can be called '**Momentus**'- Action in a moment to save us. Similarly, when you observe someone's words or actions that could potentially trigger negative behaviour in you, apply a similar tactic of quickly engaging your brakes and redirecting your path to avoid any harmful consequences.

'Momentus' effectively diverts the mind's attention before it gets into emotional embroil by engaging it into something logical or exciting. It can be engaging the mind about the next important job during the day as per your 'To Do list' for today or thanking God for any win that you had today. While doing so, one can softly think of moving away from the present location to cut away from the environment and engage in doing something productive as per your task list. Whenever you apply

'Momentus' successfully, pat yourself, as you only know how you came out of it without getting triggered. Regular application of 'Momentus' will give you the feeling of successfully manoeuvring yourself and being on the right track.

An Example:

At a weekend party at a friend's place, a discussion ensues for the coming state election—opinions about the different party and their political agenda crop up. The present government's functioning is also discussed. Somebody observes your silence and asks you to share your opinion. You didn't show interest in participating in the discussion. You said, "I do not follow political news nowadays." On this, someone says. "He is a nerd and a boring person." On hearing this, a reaction impulse arises, and you are about to give your piece of mind. At that moment, 'Momentus' kicks inside you. You apply breaks on your emotions and divert your mind to some pending work at home or thinking about the material for preparing a presentation for the upcoming review meeting. This is like a sudden disconnect and changing your course without making it too obvious.

The following steps may be used:

1. Developing an aware mind: the self-image process dealt with in the book already develops mind awareness.
2. Think about the reasons for your negative behaviour. It can be someone in the past discrediting you, telling lies to you, showing anger, frustration, or acts of betrayal or other negative behaviour
3. List them on a paper.
4. Visualize incidents that trigger negative behaviour and identify the words that provoke it.

5. While visualizing, observe where you need to apply 'Momentus' to come out clean and peaceful.
6. Again, Visualize the incident from the start and apply 'Momentus' before getting triggered. Practice it regularly.

   Every day, before retiring to bed, recall incidents during the day when you crossed the red zone or were about to cross it. Visualize the whole incident and apply the above steps. Note it down in your Attitude journal. Consistency is vital in achieving desired results.

Mind your self-talk

It is a well-known saying that:

One who knows how to regulate his thinking will know how to control his mind.

The human mind tends to engage in internal dialogue throughout the day, which can be particularly active during idle or thoughtful moments before, during, and after every action. It's important to recognize the nature of this internal communication and assess whether it's positive or negative for one's self-image. If it's negative, it should be dismissed quickly so that it does not occupy our minds and form mental impressions.

Here again, we engage the services of our observer mind to keep our thought process positive and aligned with our fundamental attitudes and set goals.

Remember the quote from Swami Vivekananda: "We are what our thoughts made us. So, be careful of what you think. Words are secondary. Thoughts live, and they travel far. Each thought we think is tinged with our character."

This means that our thoughts shape our identity and determine who we are. It emphasizes the importance of being mindful of our thoughts, as they profoundly impact our lives. Thoughts influence our actions and decisions. The quote also suggests that our thoughts reflect our character and that each thought we think is infused with our unique personality and worldview. Therefore, it is crucial to be conscious of our thoughts and ensure that they are positive, constructive, and aligned with our values.

I keep questioning, "Does this thought or behaviour help me to become what I want to be?" Use the 'Maker–Checker' mechanism to keep yourself on the path to attaining a positive and high self-image. Do not pay heed to negative behaviour or emotions arising in you. Do not disdain them even. Respect them and allow them to go gently. Focus on positive thoughts and energy. The negatives get shed away with time.

We face negative thoughts coming into our minds in several situations and almost every day.

An Example:

Take the previous example discussed under the heading – Being an observer of the mind, where a political discussion ensues during a friend's party where 'Momentus' comes in to save you from a negative emotional response. later, since the thought disturbed you, the conversation may crop up in your mind and may trigger some negative emotions. These unnecessary thoughts should not occupy your mind. Therefore, you apply the 'Maker-Checker' mechanism for the thought.

You: "I should have given a befitting reply to them. I regret missing it."

Maker-checker: "How will being angry during the conversation help your self-image?"

You: "They will realise they should not talk to me or anyone like this. It affects my self-pride."

Maker-checker: "A discussion unrelated to your field of work should not impact your self-esteem. When you respond to or pass judgment on others negatively, those remarks can linger with them, creating a bitter experience for both parties involved. An inconsequential comment or discussion should not be given undue importance. Instead, losing your composure and harbouring negative thoughts about others can hinder your efforts to build a positive self-image and affect your overall energy."

You: "Okay. I must drop this discussion from my mind and the negative thoughts that brew up inside me. I should avoid losing my composure and time for such discussions. I have a lot of meaningful things to do."

Another example:

Have you ever experienced presenting a paper or performing on a stage or field, and, despite your excellent effort, you had an unsettling feeling when some of your colleagues gave a cold or no response to your performance? You may wonder, "Did I miss a few crucial points I wanted to convey to my audience, or did I go overboard?" This regret can be frustrating, especially when you recall the points you had thought of saying but failed to mention during your speech. It can lead to an internal dialogue where you question your ability to deliver a comprehensive presentation that covers all the relevant points.

When you appear in any exam or competition, and your friend does better than you or your friend gets a better job, or someone you know has just bought a beautiful house or a car. What kind of feelings do you get in the first instance? Do you feel you could have done better than you did in the past? Do you start ruing on the opportunities that you lost? If yes, then you are already rating yourself less. Negative feelings about self gets seeded, and though that feeling may subside from your active conscience after some time, the seed that is sown takes root.

It is essential to immediately discard negative feelings and cultivate positive emotions for those who have just achieved something remarkable.

You: I regret missing some good opportunities in the past. I should have worked hard and focused more at that time. Maybe my poor habits let me down.

Maker-checker: How do dwelling on the past and regretting help you?

You: They were lucky to get such beautiful results. I've been making a concerted effort to change my laid-back attitude towards my career. Despite my efforts to motivate myself and take proactive steps toward my goals, it often feels like I'm facing an uphill battle, as if there are forces at play that are beyond my control. Sometimes, it seems as though I'm not aligned with the universe—or perhaps even God.

Maker-checker: Instead of brewing negative feelings inside you, sincerely Focus on your strengths and weaknesses and work on them.

You: I understand, but missed opportunities keep holding me back.

Maker-checker: Think about the positive things that have happened to you to date, and be grateful to the Almighty for all that you have. Think positively about everyone. Negative feelings about others can harm your self-image and progress. Let them go! Focus on your career and life ahead.

You: Agree. Whatever I have achieved so far is also a blessing from God. If I focus on myself and use my time properly, I can achieve my goals. Thank you, Maker-checker.

To prevent yourself from losing focus and getting trapped in endless striving, begin questioning each expenditure of your resources—time, money, attention—by asking, **"Is this adding value, and is it aligned with how I want to live my life**?" Let go of anything that doesn't pass this test.

The maker–checker mechanism keeps you on track.

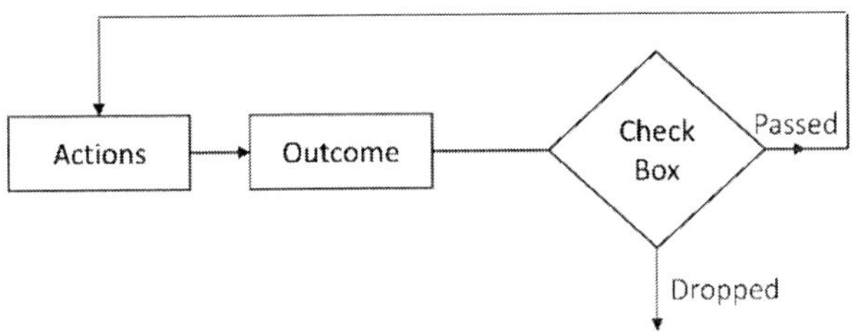

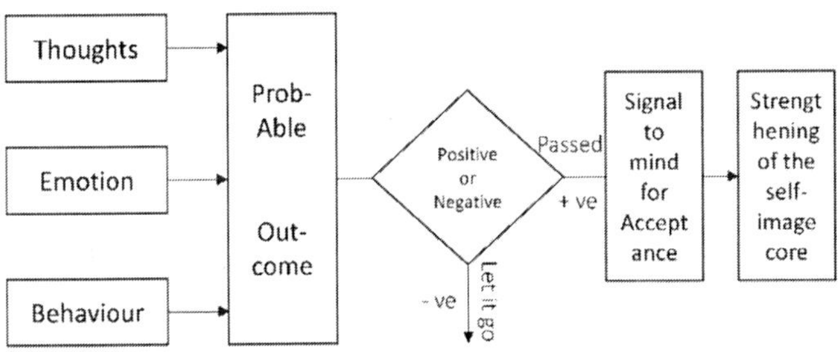

Maker Checker Mechanism

[Fig 9]

Exercise:

1. At the end of each day, write how often you encountered a 'Momentus' situation.

___

___

___

2. Against each of them, write how you dealt with it.

___

___

___

3. For every occasion you faltered, deposit 1 dollar or 50 rupees into a box labelled 'I am improving'. The custody of the box should be with your family or with the partner you are living with. At the end of every week, check the amount and resolve to improve yourself from the next moment onwards.

___

___

___

Behaviour, Thought and Emotion (BTE) Control Chart at the end of each day [For 8 weeks]. *See next page*

Weekly BTE Control Record Form

What am I committing to do? [Daily]

How am I improving? [Weekly]

Sr. No 1: I should not let unhelpful thinking habits take control of my mind and not allow these thinking habits to take us away from the present moment, so that I can be fully aware of the present moment and take appropriate actions if required. Be an observer of the mind and be mentally, physically and emotionally aware.

Sr. No 2: I meditate and affirm to be positive every day. I visualise my goals in as much detail as possible.

Sr. No 3: I am aware of the effect of positive events on my mind and body. List all positive events in the day-week and drop the negative ones.

Day	Event Description	Observations [Applied Momentus/Maker Checker]
Monday	1. DI slip rejected by the bank manager. 2. Office work didn't go well, as unnecessary jobs came up, and there were some unpleasant remarks made by seniors. 3. I was Unable to go to the gym as I had to go	1. I Could not control my mind as it went to emotional reasoning. I will have better control on my emotions. 2. Could speak out to the seniors with the right intent. Applied the Maker-

	to the market for house-related work. Feeling low.	checker at the right time. 3. Unless necessary, do not deviate from the routine set in the morning.
Tuesday		
Wednesday		
Thursday		
Friday		
Saturday		
Sunday		

Checking In: What have I learned about myself this week? What would I like to continue doing? What would I like to shift (if anything) based on what I noticed about myself?

Record: Keep a record for every week and see how you are improving.

Process for formation of a new Image Core [Summarising the Steps]

1. *Develop a progressive mindset and firmly believe in transforming your subconscious mind.*
2. *Understand the functioning of self-image and how vital it is to have a high self-image.*
3. *Get awareness about self. Understand the barriers and negative patterns that have been hindering your personal growth. Forgive every person and place that has given you painful experiences.*
4. *Release your negative attachments: The process emphasizes releasing past grievances and forgiving those who have caused hurt or have belittled you. Disconnect with your past. If, for some reason, your past has not been glorious, disconnect with your past people and places who judged you negatively.*
5. *Bring mindfulness into your daily routine: Start with 15 minutes of meditation. During meditation sessions, feel God's care and protection around you.*
6. *Visualize your Image Core.*
7. *Have the feeling of complete surrender. Get to a state of dissolution. Loosen yourself and 'let go' of all your negative attitudes and behaviours identified during self-awareness.*
8. *Keep practising it regularly till the heaviness inside you goes away.*
9. *Celebrate your new birth on this planet. If you have a guru, take his good wishes and blessings.*
10. *Develop the base of the image core with a fundamental attitude of open acceptance, non–judgment and patience.*

11. *Use the 'Momentus' and 'Maker-Checker' mechanism to develop this daily.*
12. *Believe every step is taking you closer to your goal.*
13. *This time, you will form the core of your mind without letting others' opinions get into you.*
14. *Write down on a piece of paper your purpose in life. What is your goal? What kind of personality do you want to become? Who do you want to help? How almighty is helping you or should help you? How large should your impact be?*
15. *Imagine your goal and everything you wrote in the previous step at least twice a day as an affirmation. Express the highest level of emotion in this.*
16. *Gradually, you will start getting ideas to improve your process and make your affirmations more straightforward and more direct.*
17. *Every day, check your emotions and energy levels. Your positive emotion level should be high from the beginning and should never dip. Try to maintain constant. Your energy level should be ever-increasing. Every small win is to be celebrated as a validation of your effort, as it will firm up your image. Always remember that forming a positive image and its maintenance is your responsibility. Never allow negative people and circumstances to affect you.*
18. *Align yourself with the universe and receive power from it. Perform all exercises along with visualization and affirmations.*
19. *Visualise your goals every day. Visualise yourself as an achiever. Start getting the feel of your achievement.*

20. *If you are not getting to steps 6 and 7, you still lack the emotion required to bring about the change. Attach more emotions to it.*
21. *Accept the changes happening in your life. Connecting with new people and going to different places.*
22. *Remember, these acquired habits are like your breath. Though your immediate challenge is to work without a break for 45 days, know that 45 days of consistent work is nothing compared to the reward you will get. It will be life-altering. You have set yourself to become a legend.*
23. *Stay away from negative people, specifically people who are negative to you.*
24. *Develop a new set of connections with people who would help you in your journey.*
25. *Follow your daily rituals and routine*
26. *Evaluate the completion of your task daily.*
27. *Keep gauging what changes are required in your tasks, such as upgrading your skills or changing your course of work or business. Innovate with creative thinking to improve your job or business.*
28. *Enjoy every step of the process.*

BONUS SECTION

I want to share some tips from my personal experiences, hoping they can assist you on your journey. These insights come from challenges I faced and lessons I've learned along the way. I believe you may be better equipped to navigate your path by applying these suggestions.

Build your Endurance

We have discussed setting big goals in life and taking massive action. However, many of us find it challenging to do so and adopt the mindset of "it's not my thing." As a result, one of two things may happen: either we do not set big goals in life and remain in our current situation, or we begin with enthusiasm by taking massive action for a while, only to later feel tired or overwhelmed by the task at hand, leading to exhaustion and ultimately giving up.

Take the example of going to the gym. If you start lifting heavier weights than your present capacity, you may sprain your muscles and have to take a long break. It may lead to disliking the process.

As discussed earlier about my frail condition, I thought I could overcome this by going to the gym regularly. I had the desire to get a fit body quickly and believed I could achieve the desirable body within six months of starting my gym routine. I would wake up early in the morning, and my workout regime was set to reach higher weights and run for a few kilometres quickly. But this thought needed the inner drive. The thought of improving my body was only surface-level thinking. My image core was differently built and could not attract these signals. I felt like my body could not endure such a change. Running for a kilometre was difficult, and I often fell sick.

Lifting weights was not possible due to my restricted right shoulder movement after a bike accident during my college days, leading me to believe that my body might not be suited for such exercises. I tagged myself as 'Not meant for the Gym.' Furthermore, I was either not taking the services of an instructor, or the instructor was over-enthusiastic about getting results fast. Consequently, there was a period of more than 10 years when I didn't go to the gym. Later, I joined yoga classes about seven years ago. One of my friends, also a teacher of 'The Art of Living', made a deal to pick me up every morning at 5:50 hrs, and together we went to a quiet place and did yoga. My driving force was that I didn't want to fall sick again, and I wanted to control the stress I was getting from my workplace. (Though nothing driven from the core as yet). Also, those light exercises and breathing techniques didn't require much power and stamina. After three months, my body could build some strength and endurance. I started to feel somewhat okay about my body. Two years back, I started going to the Gym. I found my present instructor there. He is a great master of building endurance, stability and power. He addressed my physical limitations and gradually helped me overcome them. It required patience and consistency.

I have been regularly working out for eighteen months. I enjoy my workouts six days a week. The endurance built through a slow step-up process has helped me continue with my gym without falling sick. However, the change in self-image has done the trick.

Every new task can be started with a very small target, especially if you are new to it. You may need to build endurance and fitness by adopting something different. Adopt a skill that may not be difficult for you but will develop your capability gradually. Like the above example, I found yoga easier than lifting weights or running long distances. Once your mind and body get set to this perceived easy skill, you may go on to do the more challenging things.

Increasing your target bit by bit, i.e., by a small degree, helps to build endurance. This increment should be small, though significant, to make you feel the increase in pressure and simultaneously feel that you are in control of the increased pressure. You will observe that you can exceed your previous set limit. Improving and controlling our actions gives us a great feeling to continue!

It is also essential that we always go forward in our journey. Do not decrease your limits. If, for some reason, you decrease your limits or you skip action for a day or two, do not look down upon yourself. Always have a picture of the star that you are. Have firm belief in yourself and faith in the Almighty that whatever you desire will eventually come to you. Each day, we should work towards being a better version of ourselves than the day before.

However, it's also important to be kind to yourself; if you are required to skip the practice for a day or two, do not worry; your self-image will make you uncomfortable enough to drive you back to the desired routine.

A star never regrets its actions and has complete trust in its abilities.

Raaj Sinha

Not seeing any perceptible change

When we work to acquire a new habit with an understanding that we have to start with a tiny target and increase it gradually bit by bit, some of us may initially get the notion of no remarkable change. After some time, a feeling surfaces that we haven't moved a noticeable bit from where we started, and we may become impatient. One may even think – I am probably not meant to do all this, and this is a waste of time, or there is some other way of doing it which I do not know. Another popular thought is that this is all meant for sissies; in business, you need mental and not physical toughness. This was a thought prevalent in the older generation and not in the millennials and Generation Z. Today's highly demanding work culture requires physical and mental fitness to tackle the challenges.

When working on a mission, it is important to understand that a significant change in state is observed only after crossing a threshold limit. Before that, no change will be visible on the surface. This is the same as boiling water. Initially, you keep adding heat, but there is no notable change on its surface. The water absorbs all the heat, and it adds to the latent heat. Water starts boiling and generating vapour only when the constant addition of energy breaches a particular limit. The key is not to leave in the middle, thinking there is no change happening. This principle applies to every aspect of life where we want to see a visible change. Keep going on! Perseverance pays.

Our effort has to be consistent and increase gradually. Every time you break the threshold limit, you see a change on the surface, whether it is building your body, doing yoga poses, meditation and mindfulness exercises, writing journals and books, improving your speaking ability, increasing your sales number, or any short-term goal that you have set for yourself.

Maintaining momentum is crucial to avoid ending up where we started. The phrase "back to square one" was frequently heard in my childhood. I wouldn't say I liked this phrase. I realized that any progress, no matter how small, requires us to keep moving in the right direction, maintaining the momentum.

Getting over the Swamp feelings

It's normal to sometimes feel negative, even when we've been trying to stay positive. When this happens, it's important not to be too hard on ourselves or let negative thoughts take over. It happens to everyone without exception. Instead of forcing ourselves to focus, doing something that brings us joy and relaxation and lifts our mood can be helpful. For example, we could take a leisurely stroll in the morning or evening, spend quality time with loved ones, play with a pet, tidy up our living space, read an inspiring article about a topic we're interested in, watch a motivational movie, listen to a podcast or motivational talk, or even play music, paint, write in a journal, etc. If all else fails, simply grooming yourself at a salon or in front of your mirror may bring a positive feeling.

Whatever we choose to do should ignite our minds and re-energise us. Taking a brief break and engaging in an activity that makes us feel good and does not negatively impact our self-image can be beneficial. This helps us maintain our progress and prevents us from sliding backwards. Such a break will provide us with renewed energy and focus.

Reading an article, watching documentaries on topics of interest to me, gazing at the morning or evening sky, being in nature, spending time with my family, or watching a movie provides me with the needed relaxation and energy.

As discussed earlier, accept things as they are and do not waste energy discussing how things should be. Conserve your energy to work towards your goal.

Do not allow negative thoughts to reside inside your mind. A positive imagination can counter a negative thought. As discussed earlier, the feeling of low and helplessness has to be opposed by a feeling of elation. Elation about your progress in the transformation journey; maybe some Jinx that you have broken, some change in your behaviour, following a better discipline or something else that you have improved.

However, if you are feeling too low, you may not be able to gather yourself to do these things. Consider going for a long walk, sitting beside a flowing river, watching the ocean waves, or feeling the freshness of sunshine and cool breeze. It is like an escape hatch to get out of an immediate negative situation into a larger universe of meaning, where you can take wing and let the turmoil be taken care of by the universe. These temporary reprieve measures by experiencing nature may put you in the right frame of mind to pull you back towards the work you love. Your vision and mission give you the driving energy. Also, you may consider increasing the frequency of affirmations.

Have unwavering faith in yourself and trust in the divine guidance of the Almighty. It's important to recognize that everyone, at some point in their journey, faces challenges similar to what you are currently experiencing. These struggles are not meant to break you but rather to forge resilience and strength within you.

Embrace the idea that every obstacle presents an opportunity for growth and learning. Each challenge you encounter is a stepping stone that can lead you to a stronger, more capable version of yourself.

Make a conscious effort to cultivate only those thoughts that uplift and energise you. Fill your mind with positivity and inspiration, allowing yourself to rise above negativity and self-doubt. By doing so, you're not just surviving—you're thriving and allowing your inner light to shine brightly. Remember, the journey may be tough, but you possess the strength to overcome it. It is inherently there inside your image core.

Getting into the right Company

The transformation process becomes enjoyable when you have a buddy or when you are in a group of like-minded individuals. Being with people driven by a sense of purpose and a desire to serve society helps us remain focused and allows us to share good ideas. However, some amount of isolation may be required at various steps in the process.

That said, it is purely an individual's decision to go about it. Many individuals prefer being alone. They need to remain more focused and purpose-driven. If you are with your family, make them aware of what you are doing to get their cooperation.

Brace up

During your self-improvement journey, there may be times when your work goes unrecognized, or people try to discourage you from pursuing it. This can be disheartening, but it's important to keep believing in yourself. Positively reflect on yourself and identify areas for improvement. Every challenge is an opportunity to improve yourself. **Don't let others dictate your self-image**. Build a positive self-image, and remember that more opportunities will come your way to test your improved version.

If people around you do not understand your transformation journey, you may not get the support you need and may have to do things all by yourself. This will strengthen you in your pursuit. So, focus on your change. Enjoy your transformation journey.

The Morning Rituals

Morning is often considered the best time to apply your thoughts positively and practice your skills. It sets up the day to begin in a fully charged manner.

When adopting these practices, it is essential to carefully select an appropriate time and location that enhances our ability to engage fully. The timing should be determined based on what best suits the individual for practice. For example, meditation should generally be avoided during regular work activity or distraction, as a calm and centred state is more conducive to the process.

If we are utilizing meditation for visualization purposes, it is beneficial to outline our goals and tasks in writing before we begin our meditation session. This preparatory step allows us to clarify our intentions and focus our minds. Once we have completed the visualization process, it becomes easier to assess how best we can utilize the day to fulfil our objectives. Should it be necessary, we can make adjustments to our planned activities to align better with the insights gained during the meditation. This structured approach enhances our meditative experience and improves our capacity to implement our visions into actionable steps for the day ahead.

To kick off your day in the best possible way, it's essential to cultivate a sense of energy and purpose before diving into your workout. Start by taking a moment for gratitude—reflect on the blessings in your life and acknowledge the power of the universe or a higher force that guides you. This practice can help centre your thoughts and elevate your mood.

Next, take a few minutes to write down your goals for the day. Be specific about what you want to achieve, whether related to your fitness routine, work tasks, or personal development. After outlining your goals, reinforce them with positive affirmations. This could include statements to reaffirm that you are capable of achieving your goals or that you have the strength and determination to succeed.

Finally, pause to appreciate your health and the unique opportunities that lie ahead. Recognise that each day offers a chance to make a positive impact not only in your own life but also in the lives of others. Embrace the power of this moment, and carry that positive energy with you as you begin your day.

This is my choice. You may have your own.

I start my day with what I call - '**GAME.**'

G – Gratitude
A – Goals and Affirmation
M- Meditation
E- Exercise

However, activities are in the order explained in the above paragraph.

For meditation choose a place that is free from excessive outside noise and disturbance. A peaceful and cosy corner of your house will be an excellent choice to practice it. To cultivate habits effectively, it's essential to create a dedicated space that encourages and invites you to engage in those practices consistently. This space doesn't need to be extravagant or visually striking; rather, it should evoke a sense of tranquillity and clarity. Aim for an environment that is free from clutter, as a tidy area can significantly enhance your focus and motivation.

Consider an easy and convenient location—perhaps beside your bed, where you can easily access it upon waking or before sleeping, or in a quiet corner of your living room that fosters peace and relaxation.

NB:

1. Avoid practising any of your habits in bed. Reserve your bed solely for sleeping. It should be a place that radiates silence and peace, which is essential for achieving restful sleep. Without proper sleep and relaxation, both the mind and body cannot recharge effectively to function at their best.
2. Always dress suitably for your practice sessions. For example, if you are doing yoga exercises, use a mat. Wear clothes that suit the moves. Do not practice in the same clothes you wore during your sleep last night or the ones that you wore for going out. If, for some reason, you are wearing the same clothes, then ensure that they are clean and tidy.
3. If you are meditating in the morning, take a shower and get ready in fresh clothes. It is not a requirement, but just an added advantage that you can introduce later in your journey
4. Switch off your mobile phones and any other gadgets that may distract you during the activity.
5. When you understand the mechanism by which the body and mind benefit from these practices that you want to pursue or are already pursuing, the benefits

received by you become multi-fold. The mind understands the process and releases the happiness hormone dopamine. We get overall satisfaction from the process and develop respect and love for that habit. Thus, the practices stay with us. It is always good to learn the techniques under an expert's guidance—one with the knowledge to explain the science.

Goals and Tasks

Write down your goals and see if they align with your larger vision, i.e. the broader objective you want to achieve. Then, see that the goals are broken down into smaller tasks. Further categorise the tasks into priority 1, priority 2, etc. See what tasks you have to take today. Assign them slots for the day. Keep a buffer slot to utilise the buffer time to keep you on track if something urgent arises or some delay happens due to unforeseen reasons.

Do some journaling or peek into social media, whatever interests you, for 15 -20 minutes. While preparing for the day, be aware that there will be some good moments and some not-so-good moments. While good moments are to be savoured, bad ones should be dropped immediately. That is how we train our minds through mindfulness to stay positive throughout the day.

Celebrating victories is important, as they often signify hard work and dedication paying off. However, it is equally crucial to embrace failures, viewing them not as setbacks but as valuable learning opportunities. Both successes and failures should be approached with the same mindset of growth and improvement.

Take the time to reflect on the lessons gained from your failures. What specific challenges did you encounter? What decisions or actions led to the outcomes you faced? By dissecting these experiences, you can identify patterns and areas for development.

Once you've outlined your lessons learned, shift your focus to actionable steps for improvement. Consider what strategies you could adopt to enhance your performance in those areas. This might involve seeking feedback from peers, acquiring new skills, or adjusting your approach to the tasks at hand.

Maintaining a continuous learning mindset will empower you to view each experience—positive or negative—as a stepping stone towards personal and professional growth. Embrace every opportunity to learn, and remain committed to evolving during your journey.

Get ready for the day with the following resolutions firmed up in your mind:

1. **Beginner's mind:** I will stay as cheerful as possible.
2. **Serving others**: I will be a little more friendly and reflect a helpful attitude toward others.
3. **Non-Judging**: I will be less critical and more tolerant of other people's mistakes, feelings, and faults. I will place the best possible interpretation of their actions with a non-judging attitude.
4. **Affirmation of strong self-image**: I am already a successful personality and will act and feel in accordance with my new personality. This new personality is the representation of my new self-image.
5. **Non-striving**: I will act in a manner full of gratitude for the success I am getting.

6. **Acceptance:** I will not colour my own opinion in a negative or pessimistic way.
7. **Trust:** I will practice smiling at least three times during the day—a comforting smile to others.
8. **Patience**: Regardless of what happens, I will act as calmly and intelligently as possible.
9. **Letting Go:** I will completely ignore and close my mind to all negative and pessimistic suggestions and acts I can do nothing to change.

Plan your day by prioritising your tasks. While on the job to complete your tasks, have an observer mind to stay positive and focused on your goals.

At the end of the day, consider where you won and where you could have done better. Celebrate your win by having a peaceful meditation or a nice time spent with your family or loved ones, or maybe you can have a nice dinner with beautiful music in the background. Whatever suits you to stay lively and energetic. Thank the Almighty for the nice day you spent. Look at the stars and feel the power of the Almighty. Prepare yourself for tomorrow.

Practice these daily to diminish worry, guilt, and negativity and improve your confidence. Do it with full faith and see the change. Gradually, make it a part of your daily routine.

This will have a beneficial and constructive influence on your self-image.

Everything that you dream of will be yours through this process.

Love you all!

END

About the Author

Raaj is an inspiring figure who has carved a unique path through life and career. Born into a middle-class family in a small town in eastern India, he experienced the challenges of limited exposure to the outside world. His early years were marked by struggle, but a profound connection to the divine and a strong sense of responsibility to alleviate the suffering of others guided him through.

Despite achieving success in the corporate realm and holding a professional degree, Raaj came to a pivotal realisation: The relentless pursuit of superficial success could lead to a life without purpose. This insight prompted him to seek a more meaningful existence that aligns with his mission to help others find their own paths.

With over 27 years of extensive experience in the corporate world, Raaj has worked with Fortune 500 companies and has garnered a wealth of knowledge in strategic thinking and leadership development. His global travels have allowed him to connect with key industry leaders and contribute significantly to process creation, systems management, and upskilling initiatives.

Driven by a passion for empowering the youth, Raaj is dedicated to transforming the lives of one million young individuals worldwide, helping them uncover their potential and turn their passions into fulfilling careers. His unique approach to achieving success, centred on happiness and purpose, sets him apart as a mentor and leader in today's complex world.

You can connect with him on:

Mail: support@raajsinha.com WhatsApp: +91 8433534152

Office Address: INFIGEN, 166, First Floor, Satara Plaza, Palm Beach Road, Sector 19D, Vashi, Navi Mumbai, Maharashtra, 400701

www.raajsinha.com